The Cherokee Supreme Court: 1823–1835

The Cherokee Supreme Court: 1823–1835

J. Matthew Martin

Carolina Academic Press
Durham, North Carolina

Library of Congress Cataloging-in-Publication Data

Names: Martin, J. Matthew, author.
Title: The Cherokee Supreme Court : 1823–1835 / by J. Matthew Martin.
Description: Durham, North Carolina : Carolina Academic Press, LLC, [2020]
Identifiers: LCCN 2020030629 (print) | LCCN 2020030630 (ebook) | ISBN 9781531018412 (paperback) | ISBN 9781531018429 (ebook)
Subjects: LCSH: Cherokee Indians—Legal status, laws, etc. | Courts—Cherokee Nation. | Cherokee law. | Indians of North America—Legal status, laws, etc. | United States. Supreme Court.
Classification: LCC KIG2013 .M37 2020 (print) | LCC KIG2013 (ebook) | DDC
347.73/2808997557—dc23
LC record available at https://lccn.loc.gov/2020030629
LC ebook record available at https://lccn.loc.gov/2020030630

Carolina Academic Press
700 Kent Street
Durham, North Carolina 27701
Telephone (919) 489-7486
Fax (919) 493-5668
www.cap-press.com

Printed in the United States of America

For C.S.M.

Contents

Acknowledgments

I would like to thank all the tribal court personnel with whom I served over the years, in particular my fellow judges: Chief Justices Harry C. Martin, William M. Boyum, and my great friend, Kirk G. Saunooke; Associate Justices Brenda Toineeta-Pipestem, Terri Henry, and Danny E. Davis; the late Judge Steve Philo; and Magistrates Hope Pheasant, Dick Crowe, Elizabeth Jackson, Sam Reed, Anthony Sequoyah, and David Blanton. It was a privilege to serve the Cherokee people, and I appreciate Principal Chiefs Leon Jones and Michell Hicks for appointing me to the bench and the Tribal Council for confirming me.

The library staffs at the following institutions have been extraordinarily helpful and patient: the Tennessee State Archives, the UNC School of Law's Katherine R. Everett Law Library and its outstanding director, Professor Anne Klinefelter, the Hunter Library at Western Carolina University, Chancellor Emeritus Anne Ponder and the Ramsey Library at UNC-Asheville, the University of North Carolina's Davis Library, and especially my research assistant, Nor Ortiz, of the University of North Carolina's House Library and Everett Law Library.

My colleagues at the UNC School of Law, the Elon University School of Law, the American Bar Association, and the National Judicial College have been uniformly supportive of this project, and I appreciate their interest.

James W. Kilbourne, Jr. made an off-handed comment one afternoon following a court session about the activities of the original Cherokee Supreme Court. That comment led to this research, and he deserves credit for sparking my interest in this period.

The following individuals have been kind enough to review portions of this material and provide invaluable feedback over the years: Andy Cahan, Judge Tim Fox, the late Justice Harry C. Martin, Craig Nova, George Sagar, George

Pappas, Ph.D., David Chase Hawisher, Clarke S. Martin, Professor Matthew L. M. Fletcher, and Col. Joe Martin.

I was fortunate to have a Ph.D. committee committed to this work, each of whom prodded me to continue it: my chair, Elizabeth A. Francis, Ph.D.; Jim Richardson, Ph.D., J.D.; John D. Loftin, Ph.D., J.D.; and Vice Chancellor Emeritus Stacy Leeds, J.D., M.B.A., L.L.M. Theda Perdue, Ph.D., helped me for years as a member of my master's committee before retiring. The late Elmer Rusco, Ph.D., served on my master's committee. Cameron Strang, Ph.D., served as my graduate school representative. Shawn Marsh, Ph.D., the director of the Judicial Studies Program at the University of Nevada-Reno, stepped in when Dr. Richardson could not attend the defense. Without their care and input, this would not have been possible.

Portions of this material have previously appeared in the *North Carolina Central Law Review* and the *Elon Law Review*. I am most appreciative of those two journals and their staffs for their interest in this work.

I am very grateful to everyone at Carolina Academic Press for their support. Thanks also to Justices Mark Davis and Willis Whichard.

Finally, I would like to thank my long-suffering family, Catherine and Clarke Martin, who have been very patient and helpful over the last eighteen years as this book came into being.

The Cherokee Supreme Court: 1823–1835

Old Cherokee National Capitol, erected 1869, and for many years the seat of the Cherokee court system in Tahlequah, OK.

1

Introduction

On the afternoon of Saturday, June 8, 2013, approximately 1,150 hardy souls braved the hot Tahlequah, Oklahoma, sun to attend the dedication of a monument honoring Judge John Martin, one of the founding fathers of the tribal court of the Cherokee Indians[1] and the first Chief Justice of the Cherokee Nation. That he would be remembered in such a significant, public way almost 173 years after his death is a testament to an enormous legacy, because Judge Martin and his colleagues created the template for the modern tribal court. Their court and those that followed established a new kind of adjudicatory process within the United States which is still growing and evolving.

The stories of that new process—a legal history—framed against a backdrop of the frontier of westward expansion and the removal of the Cherokees from their ancestral homeland, reveal a court of competent jurisdiction whose actions are understandable today but remain largely unknown in the legal community. This absence, particularly as a reference point for federal courts in assessing the retained sovereignty of the Indian tribes, has contributed to conclusions by those courts which are subject to challenge. Additionally, these stories stand on their own; they add nuance and depth to our understanding of the Cherokee Nation during its republican period up to the removal. They are the first entries in a legal history which is still being written.

A Manifest Destiny

Following independence, the nascent American republic grappled almost immediately with the status of the Indian tribes and its own insatiable hunger for land. John Gast's painting "American Progress," that nineteenth century angelic archetype of hemispheric American imperialism, "appeared as an angel of another sort" to Native Americans.[2] Ironically, at the very moment that popular democracy began its explosive rise, not only as a doctrine but also as a "style of politics," the United States "engorged" itself on Indian lands in an insatiable westward encroachment, subjugating, stealing, and slaying.[3]

> The victors then pushed the vanquished aside. Those who regretted the violence wished the process of dispossession to proceed as painlessly as possible. [Thomas] Jefferson captured this humanitarian impulse in comments to a gathering of Native Americans at the end of his presidency: "We wish you to live in peace, to increase in numbers.... In time you will be as we are: you will become one people with us: your blood will mix with ours."[4]

That the fledgling democracy would crush indigenous peoples seemed to outrage only a small minority of American citizens.[5] Instead, "against the background of Americans' self-perceived vocation as torchbearers of republicanism and democracy—at a time when democracy was still unique to their own country and the world still seemed far from safe for republicanism—the apparent paradox made perfect sense."[6]

Conquest, both of nature and the indigenous peoples within it, thus served as a feature of the "moral unity of Atlantic civilization."[7] The will to dominate received legitimacy from "faith in a progressive human drama to be played out on the North American continent."[8] Dominance by conquest rooted itself in nineteenth-century American consciousness.[9] But regardless of the moral foundations of the new nation and its Manifest Destiny, American Indians fought vigorously in various ways. These included passive resistance, negotiation, cultural assimilation, and open warfare.[10]

Governmental efforts to remove Southeastern Indians beyond the Mississippi River in the 1820s and 1830s are a natural consequence of the concept of conquest; coalescing into an organized colonial policy response to the clamor of the frontier.[11] During the nineteenth century, American Indians avoided conquest despite the dedication of the full resources of the new American republic to their subjugation, including what can only be described as germ warfare, ethnic cleansing, and genocide.[12]

Conquest and subjugation permeated the society as the new country, fresh off its second victory over the British, turned in earnest towards the native population. Even the Supreme Court of the great Chief Justice John Marshall was not immune, resorting to the ecclesiastical concept of dominance by conquest when pressed to explain the legalities of land titles involving tracts occupied by American Indians in a way that the increasingly dominant culture could understand.[13] In a remarkably open decisional process, Chief Justice Marshall admitted that the Court was, in the absence of constitutional direction, making up the law as it went along:

> That law which regulates, and ought to regulate in general, the relations between the conqueror and conquered, was incapable of application to a people under such circumstances. The resort to some new and different rule, better adapted to the actual state of things, was unavoidable.[14]

These two sentences, perhaps more than any others, accurately describe the development of federal Indian law over the past two centuries.[15]

The notable resilience of American Indians, and indeed their very survival, often leads to confusions of jurisprudence at the federal level as Congress and the Supreme Court struggle to explain exactly their legal status, the "actual state of things" or "the current state of affairs" implicit within our constitutional framework.[16] As Professor Frank Pommersheim points out, this is because Indian tribes are extra-constitutional in nature: they pre-date the Constitution and are obviously not included within it in the sense of being subject to it.[17] Indian people survived various attempts at extirpation,[18] and they persist—now fully American, but also situated uniquely within the fabric of the republic.[19]

The decades following the removal of many of the Southeastern Indians to Arkansas and what would become Oklahoma were marked by struggles to survive and adapt both to a rapidly changing world and to congressional policies that sought to accomplish Jefferson's dream of assimilation.[20] Congressional policy intended to eradicate "Indianness" by forcing boarding school education to inculcate the dominant culture, by eliminating Indian lands, and by encouraging the dilution of ethnicity.[21] Efforts to eradicate established tribal systems of justice continued as well.[22] If *Ex Parte Crow Dog* reflected the Supreme Court's late nineteenth century desire to wash its hands of tribal court issues,[23] then *Talton v. Mayes* demonstrated (before the end of the nineteenth century) that questions surrounding tribal court jurisdiction would continue nonetheless to reach the high court.[24] The Cherokee Nation's judicial branch closed as a result of the implementation of the Curtis Act[25] in 1898.[26]

During the first few decades of the twentieth century, for most American Indians, tribal governmental structures, including notions of jurisprudence, necessarily took a back seat to a more immediate concern: survival.[27] Only in 1917 was the Commissioner of Indian Affairs "finally able to declare that more Indians were being born than were dying."[28]

A Legal Framework Emerges

Undoubtedly, traditional methods of problem solving continued—disputes had to be addressed. The early twentieth century saw the renaissance of the Navajo Courts—in which ancient, venerable institutions evolved into recognizably modern tribunals, paving the way for other tribal courts.[29] This development, coupled with the evolution of a new, late twentieth century congressional policy towards American Indians—neither fully enlightened nor even benign, but thankfully no longer openly genocidal—led to new pressures for the Supreme Court.[30] These pressures include defining the sovereignty of the various Indian tribes over Indian Country and the roles of the tribal courts in exercising their aspect of that sovereignty: jurisdiction.[31]

In a series of cases beginning in 1978 with *Oliphant v. Suquamish Tribe*,[32] the Supreme Court repeatedly returned to the foundation laid by Chief Justice Marshall, reiterating the notion that "the tribes were incorporated into the territory of the United States and accepted the protection of the Federal Government."[33] Therefore, the logic went, the tribes "necessarily lost some of the sovereign powers they had previously exercised."[34]

> The sovereignty that the Indian tribes retain is of a unique and limited character. It exists only at the sufferance of Congress and is subject to complete defeasance. But until Congress acts, the tribes retain their existing primeval powers. In sum, Indian tribes still possess those aspects of sovereignty not withdrawn by treaty or statute, or by implication as a necessary result of their dependent status.[35]

This analysis led the Supreme Court to hold that tribal judicial power is constrained to the extent that it must be consistent with the tribe's dependent status.[36]

Today "dependent status" remains a shifting term in assessing the sovereignty of the Indian Nations.[37] For example, when the Navajo tribal courts punish tribal members for violating the Tribe's criminal laws, the tribal courts are exercising a "part of the Navajo's primeval sovereignty, [which] has never been taken away from them, either explicitly or implicitly."[38]

On the other hand, the Supreme Court has also determined that tribal courts may not attach criminal jurisdiction over non-Indian citizens of the United States.[39] In reaching this conclusion, the Court broadly surveyed treaties between the various Indian Nations and the United States, analyzed congressional policy, and determined that prosecution of non-Indian citizens is inconsistent with dependent sovereign status.[40] Following *Oliphant*, the Court and the Congress have struggled with each other over the question of whether tribal courts may prosecute members of other tribes.[41]

The law is equally opaque in the civil arena. The Court is unable to anchor its jurisprudence in sands which seem to shift continually.[42] To this day, no one is able accurately to articulate a framework for the exercise of tribal judicial power within the constitutional scheme.

Since 1978, *Oliphant* and its progeny have created a forty-year-long schism during which the Supreme Court has constrained the exercise of tribal sovereignty.[43] This is arguably contrary to congressional policy in that it restricts the jurisdiction of tribal justice systems in criminal and civil cases as well as in administrative matters.[44] This extraordinary series of cases creates a situation whereby tribal courts have general subject matter jurisdiction over most of their territory, but restricted personal jurisdiction.[45] The ultimate effect of this federal common law created by the Supreme Court has been the evolution of a deadly paradox: a recognition of territories that are sovereign yet effectively lawless, at least for some individuals.[46]

An almost annual uncertainty prevails, as practitioners and jurists in Indian Country await the latest pronouncements from the Supreme Court. At least in part, the core of the problem has been the Supreme Court's inability to formulate a reliable set of assumptions as to what tribal court actions are consistent with a particular tribe's dependent status.[47] Multiply this by 574 federally recognized Indian tribes and the scale of the dilemma becomes more obvious. All this judicial wrangling results from the faulty premise of *Oliphant* that the Indian Nations did not historically exercise jurisdiction, as it is understood in the modern context, over white citizens of the United States.[48]

The Supreme Court of the United States has missed an opportunity to evaluate "the actual state of things" as articulated by Chief Justice Marshall.[49] Because neither *Oliphant* nor its progeny, both criminal and civil, reference the operation of the Cherokee Supreme Court from 1823–1835,[50] the Court has understood neither the weight nor significance of tribal court jurisprudence in the early nineteenth century.[51] This has resulted in a failure by the Supreme Court to appreciate the precedents of early nineteenth century tribal courts with regard to the calculations of *Oliphant* and *Montana v. United States*,[52] the cases that established the template for tribal court jurisdiction. Those precedents are remarkable because, if properly considered, they are powerful evidence of the independence of the original tribal court. The Supreme Court has never considered this competency.

The Cherokee Supreme Court was created by the Cherokee Nation's laws and incorporated later into its 1827 Constitution.[53] The Cherokee Supreme Court lent sophisticated stability to the Nation's "social order [which] was more advanced than that of many of the rude white settlements around [it]."[54] Other than treaties, the decisional history of the work of the Cherokee Supreme Court and its constituent lower courts is the only direct indicator, the only primary historical evidence, of the exercise of judicial power, as we understand it in the modern context, by an Indian tribe prior to the removal of most Southeastern Indian tribes to the Indian Territories.[55] An analysis of the Cherokee Supreme Court prior to removal thus provides clear evidence, within a formalistic rubric familiar to the modern lawyer or jurist, of the sovereign judicial power retained by the Cherokees to this day.[56]

In *Cherokee Nation v. Georgia* (1831), the Supreme Court of the United States determined that the various Indian Nations were "dependent sovereign nations."[57] But at the very time *Cherokee Nation v. Georgia* was written, the Choctaw and Cherokee court systems exemplified the actual exercise of constitutional judicial power by a dependent tribal sovereign.[58] Thus, according to its own precedent, the current Supreme Court should look to the example of the Cherokee judges of the early nineteenth century when it investigates what jurisdictional powers have been retained by the various tribes—tribes in general, Cherokees in particular—consistent with their status as dependent sovereign nations. It has not.[59]

The best evidence of retained tribal sovereignty involving the judicial power is not a survey of treaties (honored more in the breach by the United States government), but rather the historical record of the actual exercise of judicial power by the tribal courts themselves. Careful analysis of this exercise of judicial authority discloses that the Cherokee Supreme Court possessed all the attributes of complete general jurisdiction as we understand it today.[60] Analysis of the "actual state of things"[61] leads inexorably to reasonable claims about "what the current state of affairs ought to be."[62]

Methodology

To place the Court's existence into legal context, this book examines certain primary historical documents. The two most relied upon are the Judgment Docket of the Clerk of Court of Cherokee Supreme Court and the *Cherokee Phoenix*. The Judgment Docket has been mislabeled by historical scholars with the shorthand "docket" for years.[63] The manuscript itself is titled "A Record Book of the Proceedings of the Supreme Court of the Cherokee Nation."[64] I refer to the document as the "Judgment Docket" because it contains, in notation form, a record of the decisions of the Supreme Court and associated proceedings.[65] It also contains some ephemeral material.[66]

The manuscript contains a record of the work of the Cherokee Supreme Court for twelve years: 1823 to 1835.[67] The organization and content of the Judgment Docket is consistent with the November 8, 1822, law enacted by the Cherokee National Council[68] providing "[t]hat the Judges of the District Courts, shall keep a record of the proceedings of all causes, evidences and decisions."[69] The Judgment Docket was written by various hands in thick, black ink.[70] Although its pages are not all filled in, the writing typically is cramped, generally suggesting frugality.[71] Some of the entries are boldly written, with such effusion that the ink bled into the opposite pages.[72]

The Judgment Docket is in the repository of the Tennessee State Archives in Nashville, Tennessee. It is a fortunate gift to the Cherokee people and scholars that the Judgment Docket has survived removal and the Trail of Tears, when so much else from the Cherokee Nation was lost. Its very existence is evidence that those who possessed it understood its importance. The manuscript apparently accompanied the papers of Principal Chief John Ross during the removal to Oklahoma. According to Malone, Mrs. Penelope J. Allen of Chattanooga, Tennessee, obtained the manuscript in a collection of "many valuable items" from Robert Ross, a grandson of John Ross.[73] Mrs. Allen subsequently sold the materials to the State of Tennessee for permanent preservation in the Tennessee State Archives.[74]

No tribe has been more studied than the Cherokees. Previous scholars have reviewed the actions of the Cherokee Supreme Court, primarily in an attempt to document the Cherokees' remarkable transformation of their culture from a clan-based society to a society grounded in the modern concept of rule of law as they sought to retain territory and avoid removal.[75] Thus historians have juxtaposed the Court's work with the fast-moving legal and political events ongoing in both the state and federal courts of the time, as well as in state and federal governments.[76] Malone, Strickland, and Perdue have categorized the decisions of the Cherokee Supreme Court to some extent.[77]

From 1823 to 1835, the Cherokee Supreme Court addressed a grand total of 252 matters.[78] This figure includes all matters that came before the Court, even when they did not require Court action, such as the filing of a will or a bill of sale for or an emancipation of an enslaved person. I found a total of 15 such matters. Excluding these, the Court considered a total of 237 cases: 24 criminal and 213 civil.[79] If a case was set over until another term of Court, I counted it again in the subsequent year. During the operation of the Court, the Court heard civil cases in every session, but no criminal cases were heard in 1823, 1830, 1831, 1832, and 1833.[80]

There were no entries all for the year 1831. It is very possible that cases that year were recorded in another fashion and have been lost. However, another and more likely possibility is that, as the government began to collapse under the removal pressure, the Court, in its move from New Echota in Georgia to Red Clay in Tennessee, simply did not hold a session in 1831. This likelihood is suggested by the proceedings in the case of *Betsy Walker v. David Vann*, a hearing which was specifically ordered for the Court session in New Echota in 1831, but which was, in fact, not held until Saturday, October 18, 1833, in Red Clay.[81]

My tally differs from the calculations reported by other researchers. Malone writes "246 cases came up for settlement."[82] He has almost certainly miscounted. For example, it is very likely that, in the year 1823, Malone has counted one case twice—*John Walker v. Joseph Rogers*, which was heard on Monday, October 13, 1823, and reopened on Saturday, October 18, 1823, when it was captioned *Joseph Rogers v. John Walker* and continued to 1824.[83] This was in the nature of a petition for a re-hearing of the same case[84] and, as it amounts to the same case, should only be counted once. Strickland and Dickson followed Malone's tabulations.[85] The hand-written tabulations have been open to some interpretation over the years. For example, Perdue counts 270 cases.[86]

One reason for the discrepancies is that the cases are difficult to decipher. Particularly challenging is the year 1825, in which cases were continued, or postponed, during the term of court and decided later in the term. This results in cases being included more than once in a single term, occasionally with different spelling for the names of the parties.

Unlike their state court brethren, Cherokee Supreme Court judges did not author written opinions.[87] Instead, the Court operated to afford both review of lower court proceedings and trial *de novo* before a jury; dispositions were routinely noted by the clerk rather than by the Court itself.[88] To determine the nature of the case in question, the researcher must analyze a notation form rather than a formal order of the Court. A typical Judgment Docket entry in a criminal case is represented as follows:

Cherokee Nation	)	
	)	Purchasing spiritous [sic] liquor from
vs.	)	a Citizen of the U. States
	)	
Elijah Hicks	)	

The Court decide that the defendant is guilty of the breach of Cherokee Law—

Although this style of Court minute entry does not match the style of written opinions by the state supreme courts of the time, it clearly resembles the notations in eighteenth century records of colonial North Carolina's Salisbury District Superior Court, *e.g.*:

No. 105
Hugh Montgomery vs. Daniel Boone
Debt.
Judgment Con___ by Avery for sum of 61.13.2 proc. Money & interest from the 20th March
1770 till paid 7 Costs—[89]

Thus, the records in the Judgment Docket look more like American trial court notations from the late eighteenth century rather than state supreme court opinions from the early nineteenth century.

A printing press was established at the Cherokee Nation's capital of New Echota in what is now northwest Georgia.[90] Following the inception of the syllabary by Sequoyah, the Cherokee Nation achieved enormous strides in literacy by the close of the 1820s.[91] The *Cherokee Phoenix* (later the *Cherokee Phoenix and Indians' Advocate*), the national newspaper for the Cherokee Nation, was ingeniously printed in multi-column format, often with one column in English and another in Cherokee, albeit mostly in English.[92]

The *Cherokee Phoenix* was internationally read and became a major organ for the Cherokee Nation's public relations effort with regard to the clamor for removal.[93] The *Cherokee Phoenix* covered legal matters, including crimes occurring in the Nation.[94] Although the *Cherokee Phoenix* did not comment directly on the work of the Court, except once to criticize John Martin, reference to the newspaper brings a rich tableaux providing context to the Cherokee Supreme Court's decisions.[95] Additionally, other historical records, including the records received by the Office of Indian Affairs, Cherokee Agency East, 1824–1881, and the correspondence of missionaries offer insights into the activities of the tribal judges of the period.

1. I use the terms tribes, Natives, indigenous peoples, and Indian interchangeably. I avoid the more widely used term, Native American. This reflects an ongoing and somewhat contentious debate in American Indian Studies about which among these terms should be used when referencing indigenous peoples in the Americas and elsewhere. The term Indian is among the most disfavored on this list, not only because of the obvious and, at times, confusing geographical inaccuracies, but also because it is a colonial label which ignores the rich cultural diversity of indigenous nations in North America. Noting its disfavor, I nonetheless employ the word Indian primarily because it is the term used by the government in many statutes and in case law and because it is simply difficult to tiptoe around it. The stigma of colonialism also arguably infects the word tribe, and it is thusly losing favor in academic circles. *See* David E. Wilkins and Heidi K. Stark, American Indian Politics and the American Political System 15–17 (2007).

2. Felipe Fernández-Armesto, Millennium: A History of the Last Thousand Years 360–61 (1995).

3. *Id.* at 359–61.

4. Michael H. Hunt, The American Ascendancy 1, 15 (2007).

5. *Id.* at 15.

6. Fernández-Armesto, *supra* note 2, at 359.

7. *Id.* at 360.

8. Hunt, *supra* note 4, at 34.

9. *Id.* at 15.

10. *Id.* at 15, 34.

11. *Id.* at 15–16.

12. *Id.* at 16.

13. Johnson v. M'Intosh, 21 U.S. (8 Wheat.) 543, 589 (1823) ("Title by conquest is acquired and maintained by force.").

14. *Id.* at 591.

15. *See, e.g.*, David H. Getches, *Conquering the Cultural Frontier: The New Subjectivism of the Supreme Court in Indian Law*, 84 Cal. L. Rev. 1573, 1575 (1996) ("[O]pinions in this field have not posited an original state of affairs that can subsequently be altered only by explicit legislation, but have rather sought to discern what the current state of affairs ought to be by taking into account all legislation, and the congressional 'expectations' that it reflects, down to the present day." [quoting April 4, 1990, Memorandum from Justice Antonin Scalia to Justice William J. Brennan, Jr., regarding Duro v. Reina, 495 U.S. 676 (1998), in Papers of Justice Thurgood Marshall (reproduced from the Collections of the Manuscript Division, Library of Congress)]).

16. "The United States has always recognized tribal sovereignty but has swung between periods when that recognition was strong and periods in which the federal government sought to limit or even abolish tribal sovereignty. This vacillation has led to conflicting lines of precedent and to limitations on tribal sovereignty resulting from past intrusions." Felix S. Cohen, Handbook of Federal Indian Law 1376 (Nell Jessup Newton ed., LexisNexis Matthew Bender 2005) (1941). *But see* Matthew L. M. Fletcher, *Same Sex Marriage, Indian Tribes and the Constitution*, 61 U. Miami L. Rev. 53, 63 (2006) ("The text [of the Constitution] does not appear to recognize tribal sovereignty except in an implicit fashion, although the evidence of that recognition is as close to conclusive as possible.").

17. Frank Pommersheim, Broken Landscape: Indians, Indian Tribes, and the Constitution 4–5 (2009).

18. Hunt, *supra* note 4, at 17.

19. *Id.* at 35.

20. *Id.* at 15.

21. Rennard Strickland, Fire and the Spirits 180 (1975). *See also* Cohen, *supra* note 16, at 81–82.

22. Strickland, *supra* note 21, at 175–76.

23. *See* Ex parte Crow Dog, 109 U.S. 556 (1883).

24. *See* Talton v. Mayes, 163 U.S. 376 (1896).

25. Curtis Act, ch. 517, 30 Stat. 496 (1898).

26. Strickland, *supra* note 21, at 176.

27. Hunt, *supra* note 4, at 17.

28. Cohen, *supra* note 16, at 1377.

29. Duane Champagne, Social Change and Cultural Continuity among Native Nations 93 (2007).

30. Charles F. Wilkinson, American Indians, Time, and the Law 23 (1987).

31. Cohen, *supra* note 16, at 756–57.

32. Oliphant v. Suquamish Indian Tribe, 435 U.S. 191 (1978).

33. Duro, 495 U.S. at 698 (Brennan, J. , dissenting).

34. *Id.*

35. United States v. Wheeler, 435 U.S. 313, 323 (1978) (citations omitted).

36. *Id.*

37. "The condition of the Indians in relation to the United States is perhaps unlike that of any other two people in existence. In the general, nations not owing a common allegiance are foreign to each other. The term foreign nation is, with strict propriety, applicable by either to the other. But the relation of the Indians to the United States is marked by peculiar and cardinal distinctions which exist nowhere else." Cherokee Nation v. Georgia, 30 U.S. 1, 16 (1831).

38. Wheeler, 435 U.S. at 328.

39. Oliphant, 435 U.S. at 209–10.

40. *Id.* at 208.

41. *Compare* Duro, 495 U.S. 676 (holding that the exercise of criminal jurisdiction over anyone other than a tribal member was inconsistent with tribal dependent status) *with* United States v. Lara, 541 U.S. 193 (2004) (Congress may modify federal common law by removing restrictions on tribal inherent authority without vesting the tribes with federal power) and 25 U.S.C. § 1301(2) (2007) (as modified with the Duro fix).

42. *Cf.* Strate v. A-1 Contractors, 520 U.S. 438 (1997) *with* Plains Commerce Bank v. Long Family Land & Cattle Co., 554 U.S. 316 (2008).

43. *See, e.g.*, Nevada v. Hicks, 533 U.S. 353 (2001*);* Lara, 541 U.S. 193; Plains Commerce Bank, 554 U.S. 316. This may be changing. *See*, McGirt v. Oklahoma, ___ U.S. ___, 140 S.Ct. 2452, 207 L.Ed.2d 985 (2020).

44. *See* Strickland, *supra* note 21, at 176; *see also, e.g.*, Montana v. United States, 450 U.S. 544 (1981); Strate, 520 U.S. 438; Nevada, 533 U.S. 353; Plains Commerce Bank, 554 U.S. 316.

45. Montana, 450 U.S. 544.

46. Amnesty Int'l USA, *Maze of Injustice: The Failure to Protect Indigenous Women from Sexual Violence in the USA* (2007), https://www.amnestyusa.org/pdfs/mazeofinjustice.pdf.

47. One commentator has suggested that a cause of the Supreme Court's inability to hew a straight line on jurisdictional issues in Indian Country is because the Court itself, as the slowest branch of the federal government, continues to examine historical events through a policy lens of Jeffersonian assimilation, not through the more modern congressional policy framework. Kevin Sobel-Read, Still Punching Holes in Tribal Sovereignty: How Modern Supreme Court Policy is to Indian Jurisdiction What Allotment Was to Tribal Land (Fall 2007) (unpublished paper) (on file with the author); *But see* McGirt, ___ U.S. ___, 140 S.Ct. 2452, 207 L.Ed.2d 985.

48. Oliphant, 435 U.S. at 210.

49. Johnson, 21 U.S. at 591.

50. The Supreme Court did look at the original Choctaw tribal court. *See* Oliphant, 214 U.S. at 197–99. However, one of the source materials relied upon for support by the majority in Oliphant is the Opinion of the Attorney General. *See also* 7 Op. Att'y Gen. 174, 15–16 (1853) (concluding that the Choctaw and Chickasaw lacked jurisdiction over non-Indians but nevertheless construing the Treaty of New Echota to contain "the most unequivocal recognition of the right of persons not Cherokees to be aggregated to the Cherokee nation, and subject to its laws"). This portion is unmentioned in the opinion. One of Oliphant's many flaws is a lack of complete resort to the full historical record.

51. Oliphant, 435 U.S. at 197–99.

52. Oliphant, 435 U.S. 191; Montana, 450 U.S. 544; *see also*, Plains Commerce Bank, 554 U.S. 316.

53. Laws of the Cherokee Nation 89–90 (spec. ed., Legal Classics Library 1995).

54. William C. McLoughlin, *Thomas Jefferson and the Beginning of Cherokee Nationalism, 1806 to 1809*, 32 The William and Mary Q. 547 (1975).

55. Oliphant, 435 U.S. at 197.

56. This does not pre-suppose that the banging of the gavel in the Tribal Supreme Court on October 9, 1823, constituted the beginning of Cherokee law, only that antecedents might be more accessible to anthropologists, historians, and ethnographers rather than lawyers. For an excellent analysis of aboriginal Cherokee law, *see* John Phillip Reid, A Law of Blood: The Primitive Law of the Cherokee Nation (1970).

57. Cherokee Nation, 30 U.S. at 17.

58. *Id.* at 2.

59. *See* Oliphant, 435 U.S. at 196.

60. Laws of the Cherokee Nation, *supra* note 53, at 90.

61. Johnson, 21 U.S. at 591.

62. Getches, *supra*, note 15.

63. Theda Perdue, Cherokee Women: Gender and Culture Change, 1700 to 1835 231 n.87 (1998).

64. A Record Book of the Proceedings of the Supreme Court of the Cherokee Nation (unpublished document, on file with University of Tennessee Institute of Museum and Library Services) [hereinafter Judgment Docket].

65. *See, e.g.*, *Judgment Docket*, Black's Law Dictionary (10th ed. 2014).

66. *Id.*

67. *Id.*

68. Laws of the Cherokee Nation, *supra* note 53, at 26.

69. *Id.*

70. Judgment Docket, *supra* note 64.

71. *Id.*

72. *Id.*

73. Henry T. Malone, Cherokees of the Old South 212–13 (1956); John L. Dickson, The Judicial History of the Cherokee Nation from 1721 to 1835 316 n.4 (1964).

74. Interview with Tennessee State Archive Staff (Dec. 29, 2003). *See also* Malone, *supra* note 73, at 212–13.

75. *See* Alice T. Colbert, *Cherokee Adaptation to the Ideals of the American Republic 1791–1838: Success or Failure?*, 12 Proc. and Papers of the Ga. Ass'n of Historians 41–56 (1992); Michelle Daniel, *From Blood Feud to Jury System: The Metamorphosis of Cherokee Law from 1750 to 1840*, 11 Am. Indian Q., 97–125 (1987); Dickson, *supra* note 73; Charlotte H. Peltier, The Evolution of the Criminal Justice System of the Eastern Cherokees 1580–1838 (1982); Reid, *supra* note 56; Malone, *supra* note 73; Strickland, *supra* note 21; Perdue, *supra* note 63, at 145, 150, 153, 175.

76. *See* Strickland, *supra* note 21, at 73–102; Malone, *supra* note 73, at 82–90; Peltier, *supra* note 75 at 156–75.

77. Strickland, *supra* note 21; Malone, *supra* note 73; Perdue, *supra* note 63, at 231 n. 87–90.

78. *See* Judgment Docket, *supra* note 64.

79. *See Id.*

80. *See generally Id.*

81. Judgment Docket, Saturday, October 18, 1833.

82. Malone, *supra* note 73, at 83.

83. Judgment Docket, *supra* note 64.

84. *See Id.*

85. Strickland, *supra* note 21, at 74; Dickson, *supra* note 73, at 318.

86. Perdue, *supra* note 63, at 231 n. 87.

87. *See* Judgment Docket, *supra* note 64.

88. *Id.*

89. Robert Morgan, Boone 91 (2007) (citing the North Carolina State Archives).

90. Grant Foreman, Sequoyah 14 (1938).

91. *See* Douglas L. Rights, The American Indian in North Carolina 208 (2d ed. 1957) ("Within a few months [of the introduction of the syllabary] thousands of illiterate Cherokees were able to read and write their own language, teaching each other in cabins and along the roadside."); Foreman, *supra* note 90, at 23–39.

92. Malone, *supra* note 73, at 158–59; Foreman, *supra* note 90, at 15.

93. Malone, *supra* note 73, at 157–58, 167.

94. Malone, *supra* note 73, at 137–65.

95. *See generally Id.*

Judge John Martin Memorial on the square in Tahlequah, OK.

2

The Origins of the Cherokee Supreme Court

The Cherokee Nation had its own lawmakers, laws, a tripartite system of government, and beginning in the 1820s, Western-style courts.[1] Naturally, historians see the existence of the Cherokee Supreme Court as a manifestation of the desire to resist further encroachment by the citizens of the United States on the territory of the Cherokee Nation.

> The Cherokees had long realized the relationship between their laws and the central issue of tribal politics, the retention of national land and tribal status. The legal system had been used as an instrument in preservation of tribal lands almost as long as the pressures from white men had forced the Cherokees to guard their shrinking domain.[2]

The creation of the Cherokee judicial system began with judges who presided over "councils to administer justice in all causes and complaints that may be brought forward for trial."[3] The first trial court sessions began on November 2, 1820.[4] "[A]s originally conceived[,] the Cherokees modeled the system after what they considered the Anglo-American pattern."[5]

By law, the Nation was divided into eight districts for the administration of justice:

1st District—Chickamaugee;
2nd District—Challoogee;
3rd District—Coosewatee;
4th District—Amoah;
5th District—Hickory Log;
6th District—Etowah;

7th District—Tahquohee; and
8th District—Aquohee.[6]

Under the 1820 law, four circuit judgeships were statutorily created to preside over circuits made up of clusters of two districts and to consult with the district judges.[7] The circuit judges were assigned more expensive and complicated cases, including murder, leading one commentator to analogize the district judges to justices of the peace and the circuit judges to general jurisdiction judges.[8] Their pay reflected the difference in duties. As of 1821, district judges were paid $25.00 per year and circuit judges $55.00.[9] In 1822, the circuit judges' pay was increased to $80.00 per year.[10] In 1828, the district judges' pay rose to $60.00 annually, but by then the circuit judges were earning $140.00.[11]

Devolving power from a diffuse, clan-based system of reciprocal cultural traditions to an alien, centralized government created unexpected problems. Cherokees bypassed their new court system and presented their disputes directly to the national authorities. As early as 1821, the Council and National Committee attempted to stem this flood of cases by creating an *ad hoc* court comprised of the circuit and district judges "to adjust and settle all such cases as may be submitted to them by the Committee."[12] Almost immediately, the national government handed over to the court's jurisdiction regarding "the circumstances of all stray horses."[13] An *ad hoc* legislative court must have been less than desirable. Stability dictated something more permanent.

The Supreme Court was created by statute on November 12, 1822.[14] It was originally denominated as "a superior court, to be held at New Town, during the session of each National Council, to be composed of the several Circuit Judges, to determine all causes which may be appealed from the District Courts."[15] Although the National Council and Committee continued to refer to the high Court as the Superior Court as late as 1824, from the time of its inception the Court referred to itself as the Supreme Court of the Cherokee Nation.[16] The Supreme Court of the Cherokee Nation commenced the disposition of business on October 9, 1823.[17]

In short order, the National Committee sought to remove all private disputes from its purview and to vest jurisdiction over them in the courts.[18] In 1825, the executive and legislative authorities guaranteed judicial independence.[19] However, judicial independence did not mean autonomy, as the Council and Committee tinkered annually with laws, procedures, and the setup of the court system, all seemingly to divert the mundane disputes of daily life away from the government as the crisis of the survival of the Nation grew.

The judges were elected by the National Committee and as is still typical today, were issued commissions authorizing them for their terms in office.[20] The first judges were John Martin, James Daniel, Richard Walker, and James Brown.[21] "None of these early lawyers had Office or Inns of Court education."[22] Lionized over eighty years later as the history-making "noble knights of the Bar of the East Side," they and their successors on the Cherokee Supreme Court comprised the vanguard of a native bar that continues to this day.[23]

"Judge John Martin was a product of two conflicting worlds."[24] Blonde-haired and blue-eyed and one eighth Cherokee, he was nonetheless recognized completely as an American Indian, by both Cherokees and white Americans, although he "easily could have passed for white."[25] Highly educated for the frontier of the times, he was also "wealthy by any standards of the day, being a slave owner whose plantations produced nearly seven thousand bushels of corn and wheat in 1834."[26]

For such a significant figure of Cherokee history, John Martin's early years have been the subject of confusion. Most scholars thought John Martin was the son of General Joseph Martin, who served during the American Revolution as Virginia's Indian agent to the Cherokee Nation.[27] However researchers have recently demonstrated that John Martin was actually the son of Joseph Martin's brother, John "Jack" Martin.[28] John Martin's mother, Susannah Emory, was one-quarter Cherokee and grew up in the Cherokee Nation.[29]

John Martin did not emerge as a political leader among the Cherokees until 1818. He apparently did not serve in the War of 1812.[30] Likewise, it appears he did not serve in the Creek War, although two of his half-brothers and his cousin did.[31]

Instead, Martin returns to the historical record, fully grown " 'five feet ten inches tall, blond and weighing 170 pounds' "[32] and "one of the ruling elite of the Cherokee Nation."[33] Martin and other Cherokees who parlayed their inherited wealth in conjunction with education, talent, and ambition into even greater riches "formed a Cherokee aristocracy."[34]

"John Martin served as the circuit judge for the Coosawattee and Amohee districts beginning in 1822," approximately the same time that he returned to live within the Cherokee Nation.[35] Although no Chief Justice was provided for in the original Cherokee Supreme Court, from the very beginning of the Supreme Court, Judge Martin acted, if not as the Chief Justice, at least as the chief executive of the Supreme Court: entering notations, recording compromises of judgments, and speaking for the Court. Usually with his name shortened to "J. Martin," and with the suffix "CJ or C.S.C.," Martin made a number of entries into the Supreme Court minute book, stepping into an area which would ordinarily be the province of the clerk. Perhaps the proximity of his plantation to the Court allowed him to be present when the other judges and the clerk were not. Nevertheless, the entries suggest that Judge Martin embraced the Court and rapidly became its public face. After 1823, at age 39, he was known as Judge Martin for the rest of his life.

Judge John Martin served on the Cherokee Supreme Court from 1823 through the 1827 term. During his tenure on the Court, Judge Martin heard 123 cases, more than half of the entire known docket of the Court. Additionally, seven other matters came before the Supreme Court during that period.

By the time of the drafting of the Cherokee Constitution, John Martin held five National positions: treasurer, circuit judge, Supreme Court judge, constitutional representative, and turnpike franchisee.[36] This did not go unnoticed amongst the citizenry. In a pseudonymous article entitled "Money and Principles" printed in the *Cherokee Phoenix* newspaper on Thursday, February 28, 1828, the anonymous "A. Cherokee" objected to the largess of the Nation being vested into one individual, no matter how talented: "[I]t was inconsistent and exceptionable in a high degree to have elected a treasurer who was at the same time a presiding Circuit Judge, a Judge of the Supreme Court, and holding a 4th executive appointment as public Turnpike keeper on the Federal Road: being one of the signers of the Constitution."[37] On Friday, October 17, 1828, Judge Martin was replaced as a judge on the Cherokee Supreme Court.[38] He had served for five years. However, his connection to the Court would continue.

On the same day as he was replaced on the Supreme Court, "[t]here appearing no other candidate, John Martin was declared Treasurer of the Cherokee Nation."[39] The next week, on Thursday, October 23, 1828, "John Martin appeared before the Committee and executed his bond as Treasurer of the Cherokee Nation, to the satisfaction of the Committee, agreeably to law."[40] His annual salary as treasurer was $350.00.[41] He would remain the treasurer until he was removed to Oklahoma in the spring of 1837.[42] "He continued to maintain the turnpike" and remained in service as a circuit judge.[43]

On Wednesday, October 28, 1835, during the final term of the original Cherokee Supreme Court, Judge Martin was pressed back into service in the case of *Nathan Hicks v. Isaac Bushehead, Tho[mas] Foreman & Jesse Bushehead.*[44] Judges Walter S. Adair and Archibald "Archy" Fields were objected to by one of the parties, so the General Council of the Cherokee Nation appointed John Martin and George M. Martin by a resolution as *pro tem* judges.[45] All objections to his dual service as treasurer appeared to have faded. After appearing and qualifying, the Judges Martin "took their seats."[46] In so doing they risked criminal penalties and imprisonment by the state of Georgia, which had outlawed the Cherokee Court system by fiat. The matter nevertheless went forward, and the case was resolved in favor of the defendants with a nonsuit, the dismissal of Nathan Hicks' case.[47]

Just a few weeks later, in December 1835, Judge Martin returned to Washington with Principal Chief John Ross and others in a delegation "in the cause of Cherokee sovereignty."[48] This mission was doomed to fail.

While Martin and Ross were in Washington with their delegation, a splinter group of Cherokees known as the Treaty Party negotiated a deal at New Echota. The so-called "Christmas Trick," was a $5,000,000.00 dollar offer accepted in exchange for the Cherokees' agreement to be removed across the Mississippi.[49] Two of John Martin's sons-in-law, George W. Adair and John A. Bell, signed what is now known as the Treaty of New Echota.[50] Despite the protests of John Martin, John Ross, and others, the Treaty of New Echota was immediately recognized by the government of the United States.[51] "With one vote more than the necessary two-thirds majority, the Senate approved the Treaty of New Echota in May 1836. President Jackson proclaimed it ratified on May 23, thereby setting the date for removal at May 23, 1838."[52]

"In March 1837, accompanied by at least one son-in-law (George W. Adair), John Martin led a group of three hundred Cherokee families overland" to the Indian Territory.[53] Martin's great-granddaughter, Cherrie Adair Moore, documented the journey: "It isn't known just how long it took the families to make the journey, but with family, slaves and live stock, and only covered wagons in which to move, it must have taken them almost three months, if not more."[54]

Some scholars have suggested that John Martin was sympathetic to the Treaty Party. At best, the evidence is conflicting.[55] While two of his daughters' husbands signed the Treaty of New Echota, thereby committing their families to removal, John Martin publicly protested the treaty. It is also clear that, once the die of the treaty was cast, Martin recognized the inevitability of removal and left for the Indian Territory before the Trail of Tears, at roughly the same time as members of the Treaty Party. His subsequent election as Chief Justice indicates that he was seen in a different light than the signatories of the Treaty of New Echota, some of whom were targeted for assassination once John Ross's party (the National Party) arrived in the Indian Territory.

In a government largely dominated by the National Party of John Ross, Judge Martin retained considerable personal significance and public relevance. Had he been clearly associated with the Treaty Party he likely would have been politically marginalized in the reconstituted government. What some may attribute to sympathy may have simply been the fatalistic pragmatism of a planter who knew the crop had failed.

Upon resettlement, the government reconstituted itself, and Judge Martin was called back to the bench. He was elected as the first Chief Justice of the Cherokee Supreme Court under the new Constitution.[56] Once again, Judge Martin set out to create a judicial branch of tribal government, this time as Chief Justice. Unfortunately, he did not serve long in this final judicial post. After just over a year in office and three days prior to his fifty-sixth birthday, John Martin died "of brain fever," as tuberculosis was sometimes known, on October 17, 1840. His death merited an obituary in the *Arkansas Gazette*: "DIED. Near Fort Gibson, on the 17th October, of brain fever, the Hon. John Martin, of the Cherokee Nation, aged 51 [sic] years, 11 months, and 27 days."[57]

John Martin was buried at Fort Gibson.[58] "[T]he inscription on the monument over his stone-walled grave recites that 'he was the chief justice of the supreme court of the Cherokee Nation.'"[59] Like many lawyers, he died intestate, and it took almost eight years to conclude his estate, as, at the time of his death, he still had significant assets in the state of Tennessee, most likely in the form of loans and other indentures.[60]

While Judge Martin was recognizable as the leader of the Cherokee Supreme Court, his colleagues were all well known as prominent members of the Nation. They each deserve some mention.

Judge James Daniel was educated in Green County, Georgia, and was raised in the southeastern part of the Cherokee Nation.[61] He served on the Supreme Court from 1823–1826. He was one of the signers of the Constitution of 1827. When sought out for his geographical expertise on the boundary between the Creeks and the Cherokees on December 6, 1829, he specifically included the fact that he was "late one of the Judges of the Cherokee courts,"[62] a distinction that no doubt added to his credibility as a witness to the dividing line between the two Indian nations. In 1830 he served on the National Committee and Council and was the first signatory below the principal chief in a published address to the people of the United States.[63] He was an inaugural vice president of the Cherokee National Temperance Society.[64] Judge Daniel died in 1838, prior to the removal. His eldest son, Robert Buffington Daniel, served on the Cherokee Supreme Court in Oklahoma in 1849, and, in 1850, became Chief Justice, one of the successors to John Martin.[65]

In addition to his initial service on the Supreme Court from 1823–1825 and 1827, on November 10, 1828, by action of the General Council and National

Committee "Richard Walker was elected District Judge of A-quo-hee District."[66] He was one of the signers of the Constitution of 1827.

Judge James Brown was involved early in the conversion to a Westernized legal norm when he was appointed as co-successor administrator of the estate of Joe "Rich Joe" Vann. In this office he was instrumental in the beating and sale of some of the estate's enslaved persons.[67] He later served as an officer in the Creek War.[68] In 1820, he assisted in removing intruders from the Cherokee Nation.[69] He headed up a detachment of Cherokee refugees on the "Trail of Tears," and participated in the reconstituted government in the Indian Territory.[70]

Walter "Wat" Scott Adair served on the Supreme Court from 1826–1835 and was a circuit judge in the Hickory Log and Hightower districts. He later served on the reconstituted Supreme Court in the Indian Territory. Judge Adair was the inaugural vice president of the "The Missionary Society of the Cherokee Nation auxiliary to the Tennessee Conference Missionary Society of the Methodist Episcopal Church" and one of the managers of the Cherokee Sunday School Society of Mount Wesley.[71] Upon direction from Principal Chief Charles R. Hicks, Judge Adair accepted appointment in 1826 to serve and report as a commissioner to the United States in defining the boundary between the Creeks and the Cherokees, as a result of a cessation of that territory by the Creeks to the United States by treaty earlier that year.[72] In 1831, he was arrested and rudely treated by the Georgia Guard before his release.[73] In August of that year, Governor George Gilmer of Georgia put out feelers to assess who exactly Judge Adair was.[74] Samuel Wales,[75] in his response to Governor Gilmer, referred to Judge Adair as "the Chief Justice,"[76] in the first such description of the leader of the tribal court.

Andrew Ross was the brother of Principal Chief John Ross.[77] He served on the Supreme Court from 1828–1830. On November 30, 1831, he was with his brother during an assassination attempt by presumed horse thieves.[78] In direct opposition to his own brother, as a member of the Treaty Party, he was one of the signatories of the Treaty of New Echota, launching the Cherokee Nation directly into removal proceedings.[79]

Also known as "Captain Spirit" or simply, "the Spirit," John Huss took his Anglican name in honor of the founder of Calvinism following conversion by the missionaries at the Brainerd Mission.[80] In 1825 he served for a year as a company leader of the Light Horse, a mounted national police force, for which he received $65.00. An itinerant preacher and evangelist, he roamed the mountains, exhorting the gospel in his native Cherokee.

Just a few months before he took the bench in October 1828, an article published in the Cherokee Phoenix on May 28, 1828 covering an execution may have articulated his judicial philosophy on alcohol abuse:

> Mr. Boudinott:- Perhaps the communication of Mr. Huss, (The Spirit,) contained in your paper of May 14, including the last words of the man who was executed for murder near Chickamauga Court House, may not be uninteresting to your English readers. I have, (with assistance,) prepared a translation, which I offer for insertion. W.
>
> TRANSLATION.
>
> I here transcribe the addresses of the man who was executed at Crawfish-town a few days since. The first address, which I give below, he requested me to write for him, when he was about to be executed. In the morning, while the sun was yet low, I penned it for him, on the same day on which he was to be hung at noon, April 18, 1828.
>
> These are his words: "This day I address you, my Uncles, that you may abandon the practice of drunkenness. Forsake all evil, ye whom I leave behind. I desire you to believe that the practice of drunkenness which you follow is evil. Follow that which is good. Abandon drunkenness. If you believe, we shall meet again. I have relinquished my sins to God, who only, I believe, is able to save me.- Do ye also the same. Truly drunkenness is exceedingly evil, for you see before you the end of my life; my intemperance is the cause of it. Therefore it is that I request you to forsake it. Do not fail to regard what I say, now that I am delivering to you my last words; for this day I shall leave my present life.
>
> To you also, my brothers, I say, follow that which is good. Regard my words. This also I say to you respecting our aged parents, still provide for their support. Do not injure them, for I had promised to support them, and this is my end; forsake them not, but support our parents as long as they live.
>
> Let this be all my address."
>
> The following address also he made when he was just about to be executed.
>
> "I have thought I will speak this day—let them remember my last words. My prayers only are present to my mind [literally cleave fast to me,] I cannot put them away. I endeavor only after that which was spoken to us yesterday.* There is nothing in my heart which does not

accord with that place of destination of which they speak. Should that be my destination, we shall meet again, if you believe. Now we are met for the last time. Truly the drunkenness which prevails is a great evil. Forsake it. Follow that which is good. Keep in mind such things as these.

I have also made a request to those who are left behind [my relatives] to forsake the evil of drunkenness. I wish they may regard it. But here is one standing by—he see us. This is all—I can now say no more."

Friends, Brethren; Let us read and meditate upon the addresses delivered at Crawfishtown, which are here printed. In his first address, made to his relations, his object evidently is to persuade them to forsake the evil of drunkenness and to regard the commands of our maker. And again in his second address he exhorts us all to forsake the evil of drunkenness. Thus it is that when God directs his mercy towards any individual, he is then desirous of forsaking sin, and such is the language which he uses. For it is manifest, that he must forsake sin who would obtain the mercy of God; for God has said in his word. For the language of the beloved Son of God is such as this; "Forsake your sins, and I will give you eternal life and peace." But all the unbelieving our Maker will banish into hell. When we read, let us remember what God has said, that if we believe it will be well with us.

This also let us remember, that in truth drunkenness is exceedingly evil: that which he [the criminal] especially exhorts us to forsake. For it is manifest that the great prevalence of drunkenness amongst us is the source of multiplied evils. For this man, who was executed, explicitly states that his intemperance was the cause. And it may easily be perceived, that, as drunkenness increases in our country so the instances multiply in which men do injury to each other. This is our greatest enemy. Manifold are the evils of which drunkenness is the source. I also, therefore, entreat you to forsake this creator of mischief.

JOHN HUSS.
May 3, 1828.

* I suppose Mr. Huss had made an address, after the trial on the preceding day.[81]

Another of John Ross' brothers, Lewis Ross, was one of the richest Cherokees. Benjamin Gold, father of Elias Boudinot's wife, wrote his brother Hezekiah in 1829 and included a description of Lewis Ross' home:

> His home is an elegant white house near the bank of the river, as neatly furnished as almost any house in Litchfield County. His family of four pretty children, the eldest a daughter of about eighteen years, attending a high school in Tennessee, appears as well as any girl of her age. Mr. Ross, a brother of the chief, has two or three large stores, no doubt independent, has Negroes enough to wait on us. He made us feel very welcome, and said he would take nothing from anyone who had connections in the Nation.[82]

Lewis Ross was appointed to the Supreme Court for the 1832 term, but he never heard a case. Instead, Judges Huss and Adair sat as a court of two.

On Thursday, October 25, 1832, the Court was ready to adjourn for the year. However, one case remained. In the absence of Judges Ross and Adair the National Committee appointed two replacement judges on Friday, October 26. Along with Judge Huss, this panel heard one case together: *A.* [probably Alexander] *McCoy v. David Minor*. The Court awarded McCoy thirty dollars.[83]

The first of these temporary judges was Major George M. Waters, a veteran of the Creek War.[84] Major Waters was educated in England.[85]

The second stand-in judge was William Shorey Coodey, one of the wealthiest Cherokees. Coodey often wrote on behalf of the Cherokee Nation and traveled to Washington as its representative. In 1826, he was appointed as a superintendent of the delegate election to the constitutional convention.[86]

Daniel McCoy and Walter S. Adair were elected to the position of circuit judge on November 10, 1828.[87] Judge McCoy joined the Supreme Court in 1833 and served from 1833–1835. He then served on the reconstituted Cherokee Supreme Court in the Indian Territory.[88]

Archibald Fields replaced John Huss on the Supreme Court in 1834. He served two years. In 1826, like William Shorey Coodey, he was appointed as a superintendent of the delegate election to the Constitutional Convention.[89] Following removal, he held various posts in the reconstituted government.

The final judge to serve on the Cherokee Supreme Court was George M. Martin, appointed *pro tem* along with Judge John Martin on Wednesday, October 28, 1835, in the case of *Nathan Hicks v. Isaac Bushehead, Tho[mas] Foreman & Jesse Bushehead*.[90] He was the son of Samuel Martin, a half-brother of Judge John Martin.[91] Following removal, George M. Martin became ill and died on a long overland trek from Oklahoma to the California gold fields in the company of other Cherokees on August 11, 1850.[92]

Initially, the clerk of the Supreme Court was not noted. The Judgment Docket suggests that someone served as clerk because when the judges made entries, they tended to sign their names and titles. However, on Friday, October 24, 1828, "[t]he Court met and formed a quorum. Present Andrew Ross, John Huss, and Walter S. Adair, Judges."[93] At that time, the Court "duly elected Elijah Hicks Clerk of said Court."[94]

Elijah Hicks was the son of Charles R. Hicks, who served briefly as principal chief in 1827 before his death. Elijah Hicks owned a store in New Echota, which made it convenient for him to serve. Indeed, he had served as clerk of the Council as early as 1821, and as clerk of the National Committee by 1822.[95] By October 19, 1828, he was president of the National Committee.[96] He also commanded the Light Horse, the mounted deputies of the Cherokee Nation. Married to Principal Chief John Ross' sister, Margaret, he was a staunch opponent of removal. From 1832 to 1834 he replaced Elias Boudinot, whose increasingly pro émigré sentiments made him unsuitable to the leadership of the Nation, as the editor of the *Cherokee Phoenix*. Apparently being convicted by the Supreme Court on November 3, 1826, of purchasing liquor from a United States citizen was not a bar to service.

Stand Watie, the brother of Elias Boudinot, *née* Buck Watie, became the second clerk of court on Saturday, October 16, 1830.[97] He ran an advertisement dated October 26, 1830: "ALL persons having business with the Clerk of the Supreme Court of this nation, are hereby notified to call on Mr. John Candy, residing in this place [New Echota], as he is duly authorized to do business for me in the Clerk's office."[98] With the Georgia portion of the Nation overrun by Americans, New Echota was ceasing to function as the seat of government because it lay so close to hardcore Georgian invaders in the wake of the gold rush in 1829.[99] Thus, Watie may have been with the peripatetic government, while Mr. Candy served as his local agent for filing purposes.

By this time, Watie was disillusioned with the leadership of John Ross. He ultimately became a leader of the Treaty Party, with his uncle, Major Ridge, and his cousin, John Ridge. Unlike the Ridges and his brother, he escaped assassination in the Indian Territory during the turmoil following the removal. He rose to be a brigadier general in the Civil War and was one of the last generals to surrender at the close of hostilities.[100]

Charles H. Vann served as clerk of court from 1833–1834. He was entrusted by Principal Chief John Ross to deliver a letter and a medallion, struck in Washington, to Sequoyah.[101] A letter to him from his brother, Andrew M. Vann, which became public in the *Cherokee Phoenix* and stirred a hornet's nest, warned him "to inform his friends that there is not a sufficient quantity of good land for them to settle on" in the West.[102] In October 1835, he accompanied Ross and over a dozen other Cherokees to Washington in a futile last ditch effort to come up with some solution to the removal pressures.[103] He was replaced by Elijah Hicks for the final term of the Court in October 1835.

These legal minds and others drafted a Constitution in a continuing effort to establish a sovereignty recognizable to the Americans.[104] The concept of the state as sovereign was alien to the Cherokees, but with the dawn of the nineteenth century "the Cherokees would take the next tentative step and begin to recognize the binding force of the sovereign's will. It would not be a sudden leap forward but one pursued cautiously by a people who realized that times had changed, and that necessity demanded new ways and new laws."[105] "The adoption of a constitution in 1827 was the climax in the establishment of a republic."[106] As part of this effort, in 1827 the Court changed from a statutorily created body to a constitutionally authorized court.[107] Article V of the Cherokee Constitution vested the judicial powers in a new Supreme Court and "such Circuit and Inferior Courts as the General Council may, from time to time ordain and establish."[108] The adoption of the Constitution completed the establishment of the Cherokee Supreme Court.

1. Laws of the Cherokee Nation 15–18 (spec. ed., Legal Classics Library 1995).

2. Rennard Strickland, Fire and the Spirits 76 (1975).

3. Laws of the Cherokee Nation, *supra* note 1, at 11.

4. John L. Dickson, The Judicial History of the Cherokee Nation from 1721 to 1835 303 n.51 (1964) (citing Henry T. Malone, Cherokees of the Old South 198 n.13 (1956)).

5. Strickland, *supra* note 2, at 64.

6. Laws of the Cherokee Nation, *supra* note 1, at 15–18. The spelling of the districts varies according to source.

7. *Id.* at 11–12.

8. Dickson, *supra* note 4, at 303–05.

9. Laws of the Cherokee Nation, *supra* note 1, at 23.

10. *Id.*

11. *Id.* at 98, 103.

12. Laws of the Cherokee Nation, *supra* note 1, at 18.

13. *Id.* at 19.

14. Laws of the Cherokee Nation, *supra* note 1, at 28.

15. *Id.*

16. *Id.* at 32; A Record Book of the Proceedings of the Supreme Court of the Cherokee Nation (unpublished document, on file with University of Tennessee Institute of Museum and Library Services) at October 9, 1823 [hereinafter Judgment Docket].

17. Judgment Docket, *supra* note 16, at October 9, 1823.

18. Laws of the Cherokee Nation, *supra* note 1, at 31–32.

19. Laws of the Cherokee Nation, *supra* note 1, at 46.

20. *See, e.g.*, Cherokee Phoenix, October 29, 1828.

21. Strickland, *supra* note 2, at 121.

22. *Id.*

23. William P. Thompson, *Courts of the Cherokee Nation*, 2 Chron. of Okla. 64 (1924).

24. Elizabeth Arnett Fields, *Between Two Cultures: Judge John Martin and the Struggle for Cherokee Sovereignty*, *in* The s. Colonial Backcountry: Interdisc. Persp. on Frontier Communities 183 (D. Crass et al. eds., Univ. of Tenn. Press, 1998).

25. *Id.* Suggestions that John Martin and other Cherokees of mixed blood were in some way more privileged or even superior to other Cherokees with less or no European heritage is historically discredited as a remnant of an organized genocidal plan to exploit differences amongst Tribal members in order to effectuate ethnic cleansing. *See* Theda Perdue, Mixed Blood Indians 97–101 (2003).

26. Fields, *supra* note 24, at 183.

27. Patricia Lockwood, *Judge John Martin*, 64 Chron. of Okla. 61, 61–62 (1986). Perdue, *supra* note 25, at 24, 29.

28. Fields, *supra* note 24, at 184. Indeed, Judge Martin was also called Jack. James Franklin Corn, Red Clay and Rattlesnake Springs 48 (1959).

29. Fields, *supra* note 24, at 185.

30. *Id.* at 186.

31. *Id.* The Clerk was formally recognized in laws passed on November 18, 1828. Laws of the Cherokee Nation, *supra* note 1, at 103–104.

32. Lockwood, *supra* note 27, at 63; Corn, *supra* note 28, at 49.

33. Fields, *supra* note 24, at 186.

34. Theda Perdue, *The Conflict Within*, *in* CHEROKEE REMOVAL: BEFORE AND AFTER 63 (William L. Anderson, ed., 1991).

35. Fields, *supra* note 24, at 187. The courthouse for the Amohee District was located at the Thompson Spring, near what is today Cleveland, Georgia. "The Court stood on a hill just south of the Spring. It was here that Judge Martin held his court." CORN, *supra* note 28, at 49.

36. Fields, *supra* note 24, at 188.

37. A. Cherokee, *Money and Principles*, CHEROKEE PHOENIX, Feb. 28, 1828, at 2.

38. *National Committee*, CHEROKEE PHOENIX, Oct. 22, 1828, at 1.

39. *Id.*

40. *National Committee*, CHEROKEE PHOENIX, Oct. 29, 1828, at 1.

41. Fields, *supra* note 24, at 188; Lockwood, *supra* note 27, at 64.

42. Fields, *supra* note 24, at 188.

43. *Id.*; CORN, *supra* note 28, at 49–50.

44. Judgment Docket, *supra* note 16.

45. *Id.*

46. *Id.*

47. *Id.*

48. Fields, *supra* note 24, at 190.

49. THEDA PERDUE & MICHAEL GREEN, THE CHEROKEE NATION AND THE TRAIL OF TEARS 112 (2008).

50. Fields, *supra* note 24, at 191; Lockwood, *supra* note 27, at 68.

51. Fields, *supra* note 24, at 190; Lockwood, *supra* note 27, at 68.

52. PERDUE & GREEN, *supra* note 49, at 113.

53. *Id.*

54. Lockwood, *supra* note 27, at 69.

55. *Compare* Fields, *supra* note 24, at 191, 194 and Lockwood, *supra* note 27, at 68 *with* GRANT FOREMAN, SEQUOYAH 246 (1938). (Noting that, as early as 1832, "There was a strong sentiment in favor of agreeing to a treaty of removal but the influence of Ross, Ridge, Martin, and others was too powerful to be overcome."); Perdue, *supra* note 34, at 68 (Observing Martin's "steadfast opposition" to a removal treaty.) and CORN, *supra* note 28, at 50 (Martin a "strong opponent of the removal.").

56. Fields, *supra* note 24, at 195; Lockwood, *supra* note 27, at 70.

57. *Death Announcements*, ARKANSAS GAZETTE (Little Rock), December 2, 1840.

58. Fields, *supra* note 24, at 195.

59. Lola Selmon Beeson, *Homes of Distinguished Cherokee Indians*, 11 CHRON. OF OKLA. 933 (1933).

60. Lockwood, *supra* note 27, at 70.

61. CHEROKEE PHOENIX, May 15, 1830.

62. *Id.*

63. CHEROKEE PHOENIX, July 24, 1830.

64. CHEROKEE PHOENIX, December 7, 1833.

65. Carolyn Thomas Foreman, *An Early Account of the Cherokees*, 34 CHRON. OF OKLA., 141, 148, http://digital.library.okstate.edu/Chronicles/v034/v034p141.pdf.

66. CHEROKEE PHOENIX, November 19, 1828.

67. TIYA MILES, THE HOUSE ON DIAMOND HILL: A CHEROKEE PLANTATION STORY 135–136 (2010).

68. THE PAYNE-BUTRICK PAPERS: VOLUMES ONE, TWO, THREE 299 (William L. Anderson, Jane L. Brown, & Anne F. Rogers, eds., 2010) [hereinafter THE PAYNE-BUTRICK PAPERS].

69. CHEROKEE PHOENIX, November 26, 1828.

70. The Payne-Butrick Papers, *supra* note 68, at 299.

71. Cherokee Phoenix, October 8, 1830.

72. Cherokee Phoenix, November 11, 1829.

73. Cherokee Phoenix, July 2, 1831.

74. Letter from Benjamin Cleveland to Governor George Gilmer, August 29, 1831; Letter from Samuel A. Wales to Governor George Gilmer, August 30, 1831, Georgia Department of Archives and History, Cherokee Indian Letters, Talks and Treaties, 1786–1838, Microfilm Roll No. 1253 (original microfilm transcribed by Col. Joe Martin).

75. Wales was one of the Commissioners appointed to establish the border between the former Creek territory and the Cherokee Nation. *See* Cherokee Phoenix, May 15, 1830.

76. *Id.*

77. The Payne-Butrick Papers, *supra* note 68, at 322.

78. Cherokee Phoenix, January 21, 1832.

79. The Payne-Butrick Papers, *supra* note 68, at 322.

80. The Payne-Butrick Papers, *supra* note 68, at 312.

81. Letter to the Editor, Cherokee Phoenix (New Echota), May 28, 1828.

82. Emmet Starr, Early History of the Cherokees 109 (1917).

83. Judgment Docket, *supra* note 16, at Friday, October 26, 1832.

84. The Payne-Butrick Papers, *supra* note 68, at 330.

85. *Id.*

86. Emmet Starr, History of the Cherokee Indians 51 (1979).

87. Cherokee Phoenix, November 19, 1828.

88. The Payne-Butrick Papers, *supra* note 68, at 315.

89. Starr, *supra* note 86, at 51.

90. Judgment Docket, *supra* note 16.

91. Muriel H. Wright, Transcribed/Annotated, *The Journal of John Lowery Brown, of the Cherokee Nation en route to California in 1850*, 12 Chron. of Okla. 177, 203 n. 40 (1934).

92. *Id.*

93. Judgment Docket, *supra* note 16, at Friday, October 24, 1828.

94. *Id.*

95. Laws of the Cherokee Nation, *supra* note 1, at 22, 28.

96. *Id.* at 86.

97. Judgment Docket, *supra* note 16, at October 16, 1830.

98. Cherokee Phoenix, October 30, 1830.

99. Perdue & Green, *supra* note 49, at 110.

100. The Payne-Butrick Papers, *supra* note 68, at 330; *see also* Perdue & Green, *supra* note 49, at 148–60.

101. The Payne-Butrick Papers, *supra* note 68, at 329.

102. Cherokee Phoenix, February 4, 1832.

103. *Id.*

104. Strickland, *supra* note 2, at 121.

105. John Phillip Reid, A Law of Blood: The Primitive Law of the Cherokee Nation 274–75 (1970).

106. Henry T. Malone, Cherokees of the Old South 84 (1956).

107. *Id.* at 83–86.

108. Laws of the Cherokee Nation, *supra* note 1, at 126.

Replica of the original Cherokee Supreme Court, New Echota Historic Site, Calhoun, GA.

3

The Language of the Court

We do not know the language in which the proceedings before this early tribal court were conducted. Transcripts of testimony in the trial of the cases are unknown. Such an inquiry, however, raises interesting and significant questions about the people who participated in the proceedings.

Recent studies converge "on a basic vision of language as a medium not only for reference to, but fundamentally for construction of social realities and orders. Thus legal interaction is a critical tool for the exercise of sociolegal power."[1] Growing scientific evidence suggests that "language shapes even the most fundamental dimensions of human experience: space, time, causality and relationships with others,"[2] each of which impacts adjudicatory models. Professor Lara Broditsky's research indicates that "[p]eople who think differently about space are also likely to think differently about time," and she has found "such linguistic differences influence how people construe what happened and have consequences for eyewitness memory."[3] Thus, the language spoken in the courtroom deeply affects the ways in which decisions are reached, including the ideology of the judge in supporting them.[4]

We do know that the Cherokee Supreme Court cases were docketed in American Legal English, a dialect of English, which suggests that the proceedings were conducted in English. Additionally, some of the records themselves indicate the proceedings were in English. For example, the Judgment Docket includes a notation awarding Archd (sic) Foreman $12.00 for translating the Cherokee language in a case. The oath of the clerk of court, "You do solemnly swear that you [ ] as clerk to this Supreme Court keep as true [ ] of the proceedings of said Court [ ] favor or truthfully to any party whosoever" was written in American Legal English.

One of the cases of the Court demonstrates a conversion to English. On September 27, 1830, Circuit Judge Walter Adair noted in the Judgment Docket that "George Baldridge came in and had the following affidavits recorded."[5] Baldridge swore that he had recently been robbed of a trunk which included within it two bills of sale for two of his enslaved persons, Silver and Hannah. Without some indicia of ownership, Baldridge risked being dispossessed. He appeared before Judge Adair along with James Spencer and Charles Dry Fore Head. Spencer and Dry Fore Head both swore they witnessed the transactions between Baldridge and the two sellers, and both indicated that bills of sale were, in fact, generated and delivered to Baldridge. Dry Fore Head also swore that he acted as an interpreter between Baldridge and the seller of Hannah, evidence which suggests that Baldridge did not speak English, or did not speak it well. He likely was not literate in English, as he signed with an X for his mark. These notations suggest that Baldridge's testimony before Judge Adair may have been in Cherokee and docketed in American Legal English.

Some back and forth had to occur. For example, the *Phoenix* reports on more than one occasion that Judge John Huss only spoke Cherokee.[6]

Sequoyah famously created the Cherokee syllabary 1821, and, while it was rapidly accepted by the people,[7] the Nation did not officially adopt it until 1825, by which time the Cherokee Supreme Court was already operational. Until that time, translation into English would have had to be phonetic only. This would have hindered translations, although it is present in the Judgment Docket in the translations of the Cherokee names of individuals who came before the Supreme Court as parties, witnesses, sureties, or in other fashions. Written language of the Cherokees was just being accepted during the time that the Court was created. Despite widespread acceptance, it never fully gained traction as the official written language of the Nation prior to removal, except in the publication of the *Cherokee Phoenix* newspaper, a semi-official organ of the Nation, which often published in both English and Cherokee. For example, it is notable that the Constitution of the Cherokees of 1826 was originally printed in English.

However, John Howard Payne reported that early on George Gist, or Sequoyah, demonstrated his written language in the courtroom.

> The first composition he put together was on the subject of the … 'boundary' line between … his own country and Georgia & Tennessee. After that, he had a … suit in the Indian Court … held in Chatouga. He wrote down a statement of his case. When he got there, he read his statement, instead of speaking; and all the people were amazed. This was about a year after the invention was completed.[8]

Written Cherokee was well known within the court system, even before the Supreme Court was constituted.

There are a number of significant reasons why the courts of the Cherokee Nation would have reported their decisions in American Legal English. The first two are economic.

The United States currency was the currency of the Nation. Payment was made to the Cherokees by the federal government in dollars. Laws of the Nation were enacted with dollars in mind. The object of financial suits was most often an award of damages in United States currency.

One of the earliest matters before the Court involved a counterfeit United States coin.[9] On October 23, 1823, Henry (or Harry) Tharpe appeared before Judge Martin and swore out an affidavit in which he alleged that on or about September 20, 1823, "a certain Cherokee man by the name of Terrapin Head traded him a piece of metal, purporting to be" an 1802 coin.[10] Upon examination, Tharpe determined that Terrapin Head had swindled him with a counterfeit.[11] Tharpe demanded redemption from Terrapin Head and sought the assistance of the Court to document it and to bring the matter "to closure."[12] The reasons for documenting the circumstances are lost but could involve putting individuals on notice regarding the counterfeit coin or in assistance to Terrapin Head in the event he sought redress from the individual from whom he obtained it.[13] The incident demonstrates that even in its first term the Cherokee Supreme Court was truly open and the judges were available to the public for all sorts of redress. From its inception, the Cherokee people recognized and accepted the Court as an independent arbiter of disputes.

With the U.S. dollar as the coin of the Cherokee realm, it is not hard to suppose that the language of economic transactions involving currency was English. Indeed, all of the itemization of witness fees in the Judgment Docket are in Arabic numbers. When money damages were awarded, they were consistently measured in dollars. The judges and the witnesses counted not in Cherokee, but in dollars. Accordingly, it becomes easier to see how contract cases would be reported in American Legal English.

A second economic reason to report the decisions of the tribal court in American Legal English was the Cherokees' desire to foster commerce. Economically the Cherokees depended upon agriculture, cash support from the federal government, and, to a lesser extent, hunting and the skin trade. Trade within the Cherokee Nation and even with the Americans was important for the maintenance of a viable society. When President Andrew Jackson cut off annual annuity payments to the Cherokee treasury in 1830 and insisted that the individual members of the Nation travel to the Indian agent to accept payment on a *per capita* basis (a pittance), the Nation was pushed closer to economic and political collapse. Tribal court judgments in American Legal English could easily be understood across cultures and thus provided an outlet for commercial disputes to be readily resolved and available as of record.

While this promoted commerce, it occurred in the context of Georgia's continued removal pressure, including a law in 1833 nullifying all contracts between an Indian and a white man unless witnessed by two non-Indians.[14] Georgia's law had the practical effect of removing contract cases between Cherokees and Georgians into the Georgia court system.[15]

A subset of this desire to foster commerce was the determination of the wealthy Cherokees to maintain the slave trade. Decisions involving the ownership and freedom of enslaved persons incorporated facts that occurred in the United States, but which were applied as a matter of law within the Cherokee Nation. The recording of these matters and decisions in the tribal court in American Legal English made the provenance of ownership clear and of record, even to outsiders.

Finally—and perhaps most importantly—a major goal of the creation of the Cherokee Supreme Court was to show to the United States that the Cherokee people had attained such attributes of Americanism to forestall and prevent their removal. The Court, in other words, represented hope as an exemplar of the Cherokee's validity as partners with the Americans in the drama being played out on the frontier. In the context of colonialism, such actions are sometimes attributed to a kind of resistance called "mimicry."[16] However, "for the Cherokee it was also a practical necessity to replicate European-American notions of land ownership by attaining attributes and practises of the dominant culture."[17] Pappas argues that this kind of acculturation differed from the "mimicry" found in colonial studies because of its duality, both as an element of resistance by the outwardly facing adoption of dominant American political patrimony as well as an inward looking preservation of centuries of decentralized social, cultural, and traditional mores.[18] The result, according to Perdue, is "that two legal systems operated simultaneously in the early Cherokee republic."[19] In the shadow, traditional system, recompense could follow cultural traditions. With this in mind, it is not surprising that the *lingua franca* of the Cherokee court system was essentially the same as the Americans'.

This conclusion is supported by a delightful piece of ephemera, laid into the Judgment Docket—the closing argument of an attorney in a hog stealing case. Although we do not know whether the document is connected to any of the reported cases, it gives some insight into the court rhetoric of the period:

> May it please the Court
> While Bonaparte is marching his army from Elba to Paris and from Paris back to Elba inundating the whole country in blood I stand here the humble advocate of this notorious hog thief. The goats may climb to the summit of those mountains. The sheep may feed on the fields below and the cattle may graze the grass off the meadow but my client are no more guilty of stealing that are hog than a toad got no tail.[20] [sic]

This document does not appear to have been translated. Additionally, there is one small entry[21] and one ephemeral scrap written in Cherokee in the materials, and they are untranslated. This suggests that when Cherokee was used, it was recorded in that fashion.

The difference between spoken and written legal thought remains significant. Moreover, although spoken law and written law clearly interconnect, spoken law has a life of its own, logic and rationales of its own that are separate from and cannot be found in written law.[22] While the evidence suggests English, not knowing with certainty the language in which the tribal proceedings were conducted remains a significant mystery.

Notably, the Americans were creating their own state and federal court systems during this same time period. Virtually contemporaneously, "[i]n establishing a legal system of their own, the independent Americans continued to use statutes, precedents, and forms—and consequently legal language—from their former colonial masters."[23] As the Americans retained English common law, it is not surprising to find Cherokee decisions relying on it as well as its precedents and formal devices in creating their own independent yet acculturated system of laws. Thus, crimes, torts, contracts, replevin, trover, wills, summonses, and other English legal constructs, all of which would have been alien to the Cherokee clan society of the early eighteenth century, found their way, permanently, it appears, into the Cherokee legal culture of the early nineteenth century and indeed now in modern Cherokee society, as well.[24] Tiersma documents similar instances in many former English colonies in Africa, Australia, Canada, India, Malaysia, Singapore, and New Zealand.[25] This appears to be the earliest instance of its documentation in an American Indian Tribe.

1. Justin B. Richland, Arguing with Tradition 62 (2008) (citations omitted).

2. Lara Broditsky, *How Language Shapes Thought,* Sci. Am., Feb. 2011, at 63–64.

3. *Id.*

4. *See, e.g.*, Susan U. Philips, Ideology in the Language of Judges 116 (1998) ("Linguistic anthropological approaches to situated language use in the traditions of the ethnography of communication and textual analysis (which show culture and ideology constituted in discourse) offer theoretical and methodological models for the empirical and practical grounding of ideology in language use.").

5. A Record Book of the Proceedings of the Supreme Court of the Cherokee Nation (unpublished document, on file with University of Tennessee Institute of Museum and Library Services) at Monday, September 27, 1830 [hereinafter Judgment Docket].

6. *See, e.g.*, Cherokee Phoenix, June 4, 1828; Cherokee Phoenix, July 2, 1828; Cherokee Phoenix, May 27, 1829.

7. Emmet Starr, Early History of the Cherokees 54–56 (1917).

8. The Payne-Butrick Papers: Volumes One, Two, Three 139 (William L. Anderson, Jane L. Brown, & Anne F. Rogers, eds., 2010) [hereinafter The Payne-Butrick Papers].

9. Judgment Docket, *supra* note 5.

10. Judgment Docket, *supra* note 5, at Saturday, October 25, 1823.

11. *Id.*

12. *Id.*

13. The latter theory seems somewhat unlikely, as Terrapin Head was a prominent member of White Path's Rebellion, which opposed acculturation with Anglo-American culture along with laws and constitutions. *See, e.g.*, The Payne-Butrick Papers, *supra* note 8, at 327, 331.

14. Theda Perdue & Michael Green, The Cherokee Nation and the Trail of Tears 102 (2008).

15. Tim A. Garrison, The Legal Ideology of Removal 120 (2002).

16. George D. Pappas, The Literary and Legal Genealogy of Native American Dispossession 190 (2017).

17. *Id.* at 191.

18. *Id.* at 191–94.

19. Theda Perdue, *Clan and Court: Another Look at the Early Cherokee Republic,* 24 Am. Indian Q., No. 4, 562, 568 (2000).

20. *See generally* Judgment Docket, *supra* note 64.

21. It appears Judge Huss signed his name in Cherokee on Thursday, November 13, 1828, in the order adjourning Court until 1829.

22. Philips, *supra* note 4, at 123.

23. Peter Tiersma, Legal Language 45 (1999).

24. This is not to say that the duality observed by Perdue has diminished. An anecdotal example is a twenty-first century story told by Joey Owle, then the Bailiff of the Cherokee Court, to the author. One night, while on patrol as a police officer, Mr. Owle received a radio dispatch to respond to a call reporting a man crying and screaming in the woods of the Big Cove community, a traditional enclave within the Qualla Boundary, the reservation of the Eastern Band of Cherokee Indians. Armed with only his service weapon and a flashlight, Mr. Owle trudged through the steep, dark woods, following the cries, until he came to a clearing, where he spied a man calling for help, tied to a stake before a bonfire. As Mr.

Owle approached the man, a number of men came out of the shadows and surrounded him. When officer Owle demanded to know what was going on, one of the men told him, "This is our fire. We were performing our traditional and sacred dances. This man is drunk and he has interrupted and disrupted our ceremonies. So, we have tied him up and are going to pray and dance for him until dawn." When the author asked officer Owle what he did, he responded, "Judge, there were seven of them and one of me. I left. I could hear that guy wailing all the way back to the car."

25. Tiersma, *supra* note 23, at 46–47.

Replica of the original Judges' bench, New Echota Historic Site, Calhoun, GA.

4

Women and the Court

Cherokee women were full and equal users of their formal justice system. Although they did not operate the Supreme Court (only men served as judges, clerks, and jurors), they fully participated in its proceedings as both plaintiffs, defendants, and witnesses. The very first entry and the last entry in the Judgment Docket were matters involving women. No women appeared in any criminal case heard by the Supreme Court. Of the 213 civil cases, 65, or 30.51%, of the cases involved females as parties. Considering all 252 matters that came before the Court, 69, or 27.38%, involved women as actors. This does not include the multiple documented cases in which women served as witnesses.

A similar comparison of the opinions of the Supreme Courts of the neighboring states of North Carolina, Tennessee, and Alabama during the same time period[1] discloses that white American women were significantly less involved in their court systems as parties. In the North Carolina reports of Supreme Court decisions, women were parties in 23.62% of all cases (273 out of 1,156 cases). In Tennessee, the numbers were fewer: 12.79% (116 out of 907 cases). In Alabama, even fewer women were represented as parties: 6.86% (65 out of 947 cases).[2]

Cherokee women participated in their Supreme Court as users of the system at a significantly higher rate than did white American women in neighboring states. Understanding this requires a cross-cultural comparison.

"Cherokee women held an amount of societal power that was stunning to Europeans."[3] Indeed, Indian culture in general seemed beyond European ken. Upon contact, bewildered British discerned nothing in the aboriginal culture resembling law and order as they understood it in London. Widespread comments echoed the report of an eighteenth-century British officer who "wrote that Indian 'government, if I may call it government ... has neither laws nor power to support it.'"[4]

If the law side of the equation seemed non-existent,[5] the order side appeared completely upside down:

> When Cherokees met Europeans, the Europeans assumed that one of the reasons that the Cherokees were uncivilized was because the women had so much power. Their power was tied to their role as producers and mothers. The Cherokee and Euro-American worldviews differed dramatically regarding appropriate gender roles, marriage, sexuality and spiritual beliefs. As we have seen, Cherokee women were farmers, and Cherokee men were hunters. Their society was matrilineal and matrilocal, which meant that the women owned their residence and the fields they worked. Cherokee women were healers, producers, warriors, traders, wives, and mothers. They taught their daughters to cook, prepare game, do beadwork, and make baskets, pottery, and clothing. They enjoyed sexual freedom and easy divorce, but the clans maintained strict incest taboos, and in all their actions tribe members had to take the welfare of the community into account. Cherokees believed in a sexual division of labor, but the difference was associated with complementarity and equality, not hierarchy or domination. Their religious beliefs differed greatly from Christian theology. Because the public and private spheres were not highly differentiated, Cherokee women enjoyed a higher status than in those societies where there is little permeability.[6]

This status allowed these women access to their court system in ways that their counterparts in America never experienced.

The cases involving women ranged from the most mundane—for example where Flose Taylor received a judgment against Caty McEntosh of $2.40 on Monday, October 29, 1827[7]—to among the costliest, for example the $2,173.69 award against Andrew Ross and Elizabeth Pack on Saturday, October 17, 1829,[8] a verdict with an approximate relative value in today's dollars of $57,800.00. Excepting criminal matters, cases with women involved the same broad subject matter litigated by men: slaves, debts, cattle, farms, trespasses, houses, horses, and hogs.

In one case the Supreme Court failed to provide the necessary safeguard protections to a Cherokee household.

> The members of a Cherokee household were usually a mother, her daughters, her daughters' children, and her unmarried sons. The husbands of the women of the household also lived with the family and contributed to its support; but since Cherokee marriages were fre-

> quently of a short duration, their continued presence was not assured. In the event of a marital separation, the husband returned to the household of his mother and sisters, while his children remained with his wife and her family.[9]

The husband "spent much of his time with his own lineage because these were his kinsman, while his wife's people, including his wife and children, were not."[10] In this matrilineal society a husband neither possessed any property right in his wife and children (as opposed to the common law tradition) nor was he actually bound to them in any relational way understood by the Europeans, whose idea of marriage included elements of contract law. Instead, he was related to his mother, her sisters, and their children, all tied together by clan identity. A husband and wife would not have shared clan membership as this was taboo.

The degree of sexual freedom enjoyed by all Cherokees astonished the British.[11] Even in the twenty-first century, such autonomy would give many Americans pause. Cherokee women controlled their own sexuality. Unmarried women freely engaged in sexual congress as they pleased, with the only constraints consisting of incest taboos prohibiting intercourse with members of their clans and their fathers' clans and taboos relating to their menstrual cycles as blood was a source of both great power as well as great danger.[12] "Married women also enjoyed considerable latitude."[13]

Husbands were generally unperturbed by the licentiousness of their wives.

> The most acceptable course of action for the husband of a wayward wife, however, was to ignore the infidelity and, if he chose, take another wife. Louis-Phillipe observed: "If a Cherokee woman sleeps with another man, all he does is send her away without a word to the man, considering it beneath his dignity to quarrel over a woman." According to Norton, in the case of a wife's adultery, "the husband is even disgraced in the opinions of his friends if he seeks to take satisfaction in any other way, than that of getting another wife."[14]

To the extent a husband did respond to the unfaithfulness of his wife, typically it was in the form of conjury.[15] Conjury (aboriginal sorcery) was employed in an effort to restore balance to the spirit or natural worlds, or, as they co-existed simultaneously in reality, both. Thus, magical

> [f]ormulas existed to fix the affections of a wife who had a wandering eye, and priests had several methods, including colored beads and divining crystals, to determine whether she had been unfaithful. If the wife proved guilty and the husband desired revenge, the priest took

> some dead flies in his hand. If one came to life upon his opening the hand, it would burrow its way into the body of the wife and bring her a painful death on the seventh day. Payne, who recorded this practice, commented: "Whether the fly received any assistance from the husband or the priest is not reported."[16]

James Adair, in his late eighteenth century observations of the indigenous population, did note one instance of gang rape revenge by the male relatives of a cuckolded Cherokee husband, but he emphasized this was an exception.[17]

On the other hand, the straying of men could be the source of significant societal disruption:

> Although female infidelity rarely perturbed men, husbands who strayed caused considerable disharmony in the community. Women whose husbands abandoned them for other women were "unreconcilable" according to Longe, who suggested that women had more of a proprietary interest in men than men had in women. He described a pattern of behavior that we are more accustomed to find in reverse in modern America: "Sometimes the young maids comes and steals away women's husbands. Then the wife, the first time she meets her, there is a bloody battle about it. Sometimes one gets the victory and sometimes the other. They that gets the upperhand carried the husband. If these two women were to live a thousand years in the same town, nay, next door, they will never have any communication together, nor so much as speak the one to the other." Since such conflicts probably drew in family members as well, the results could be terribly disruptive. Such difficulties, however, never became the town's concern; they remained personal and familial.[18]

However, the case of *Elizabeth Pettit v. James Pettit*[19] such behavior became the concern of the entire Nation. Initially the case arose in the newspaper. On January 14, 1829, James Pettit took out the following classified ad:

> WHEREAS my wife ELIZABETH has, without any cause whatever, absented herself from my lodgings, all persons are hereby cautioned against harboring and protecting her, or forming any bargains or contracts with her, as the subscriber, is determined not to be responsible for them.[20]

Upon viewing this, Mrs. Pettit fired off a letter to the editor:

> Dear Sir: In your last number, I find where my husband James Petit advertises me for being absenting myself from his lodgings without any cause and cautions all persons from harboring or protecting me or forming any contracts with me, as he is determined not to pay any of my contracts. Sir, I must let a generous public know my reasons for leaving his lodging. I did it when I was ordered. I did not carry away any of his keys. I was compelled to do what I have done—he has killed nearly all of my stock, for which I shall want pay. You will please give this an insertion in your paper, and oblige an injured woman.[21]

Mortified at this exchange, and in a sign of things to come, Elias Boudinot, the editor of the *Phoenix*, declared that, henceforth "no advertisement similar to the one complained of above will be inserted in the Phoenix, except when the advertising person produces good reason to the editor to show that he or she has just cause of complaint."[22]

The lawsuit for killing the livestock was heard by the Supreme Court on Wednesday, October 14, 1829, at which time Mrs. Pettit won a verdict of $64.00 "in young cattle to be paid at valuation."[23] The execution was issued on October 20, 1829.[24]

This was not enough. In the eyes of the community, Pettit, a white man, had humiliated his wife and forced her from the marital home. Among other things, he had taken up with another wife. Bigamy was illegal in the Nation,[25] and it was specifically illegal for white men to have more than one Cherokee wife.[26] His actions created disharmony.

Two weeks after the Supreme Court verdict on Wednesday, October 28, 1829, on motion of James Martin, the National Committee, apparently unsatisfied, issued a warrant directing the marshal to arrest and bring James Pettit before the body. When the marshal drug Pettit before the National Committee, he was arraigned on charges of bigamy and mistreating his Cherokee wife, Elizabeth Pettit.[27] A summary trial before the Legislative Council immediately ensued, where the Supreme Court's verdict was augmented significantly. "[I]t was decided that Mrs. Pettit had a sufficient provocation to leave Mr. Pettit's house."[28] Additionally, Pettit was fined $500.00, and ordered removed from the plantation in favor of Elizabeth.[29] Acting swiftly, the marshal had Pettit's crops, cattle, and an enslaved person named Gabriel up for sale to satisfy the fine, which was to inure to the benefit Mrs. Pettit.[30]

It cannot be a coincidence that, on November 2, 1829, the principal chief signed a new law into effect:

> *Whereas*, It has long been an established custom in this Nation and admitted by the courts as law, yet never committed to writing that the property of Cherokee women after their marriage cannot be disposed of by their husbands, or levied upon by an officer to satisfy a debt of the husband's contracting, contrary to her will and consent, and disposable only at her option—therefore,
>
> *Resolved by the National Committee and Council, in General Council Convened*, That the property of Cherokee, and other women, citizens of this Nation, after their marriage shall not be taken or disposed of in any manner contrary to her consent, for the purpose of satisfying a debt contracted by her husband, nor shall the property of the husband be liable to seizure, or otherwise to satisfy the debts contracted by the wife.[31]

Episodes such as this demonstrate that Cherokees possessed (and still continue to possess) a great dedication to the maintenance of the community; the prevailing ethic being one of harmony.[32] "Furthermore, clans helped them live upstanding lives through instruction, support, and protection. Clans enabled Cherokees to place themselves in the world and establish appropriate relationships with the rest of the cosmos."[33]

This could not have been farther from the experience of the early Americans, whose Anglo legal framework was premised upon a strategy of winners and losers.[34] While disentangling a marriage in America, with all of its attendant property rights, remained an onerous, often impossible task,[35] the Cherokees' harmonious balance led to easy divorce.

> Consequently, the Cherokees normally resolved sexual rivalries through divorce and remarriage. Louis-Phillipe claimed that an Indian man who had several wives "takes them on and turns them away like servants, and similarly they leave him when it suits them to do so." Although many Cherokee marriages endured a lifetime, some ended in less than a fortnight, and Timberlake maintained that a few Cherokees changed spouses three or four times a year. Adair placed the blame for the instability of Cherokee marriages squarely on the women. "Their marriages are ill observed, and of short continuance; like the Amazons, they divorce their fighting bed-fellows at their pleasure, and fail not to execute their authority, when their fancy directs them to a more agreeable choice." The Cherokees attached no stigma to those who dissolved their marriages. When Alexander Longe inquired about the reason for the divorce of a Cherokee couple, a priest

> told him "that they had better be asunder than together if they do not love one another but live for strife and confusion." In a similar vein, an Indian attempted to explain his people's philosophy of marriage to Adair: "My Indian friend said, as marriage should beget joy and happiness, instead of pain and misery, if a couple married blindfold, and could not love one another afterwards, it was a crime to continue together, and a virtue to part and make a happier choice."[36]

The English and Americans found the societal order they encountered in the Cherokee people both baffling and disturbing. Not only did the sexual freedom enjoyed by Cherokee women completely upend the Anglo/Teutonic concepts of women as chattel, these freedoms permitted the Native women to participate fully in their own government at the highest levels. Adair observed this alien behavior to be completely extraordinary. "The Cheerake [sic] are an exception to all civilized or savage nations, in having no laws against adultery; they have been a considerable while under petticoat-government, and allow their women full liberty to plant their brows with horns as oft as they please, without fear of punishment."[37] Adair employed a double entendre: while he expresses dismay that women can wear the horns of the cuckold, he also is referring to their position within Cherokee society. In Adair's time, chiefs, headmen, and other civic leaders beyond the frontier were referred to as " 'wearing horns,' " an allusion to the days when such officers wore actual antlers.[38] Thus, Adair expressed his amazement that women could lead the society with no backlash or punishment from the men.[39]

The "hidden" judicial system argued by Perdue[40] could be deployed to balance equities in the dissolution of a marriage. In this way, the outward-facing Supreme Court had an internal cultural safety valve.

These kinds of structures exist in twenty-first century tribal courts. Western commentators almost universally view them negatively, as the ability to seek alternate recourse at the tribal council or otherwise in the community is viewed as undermining both the rule of law and the independence of the judiciary. These commentators miss the point: notwithstanding their drag on judicial institutions, such traditions and customs serve to preserve normative indigenous expectations and to redirect outcomes in a more understandable or meaningful way for users of the systems. In the case of Elizabeth Pettit, this included re-elevating her status to equal that of her husband.

The evidence suggests that such a safety valve was not automatic; instead, the proper circumstances had to exist in order to activate it. For example, on November 10, 1828, Nancy Boggs came before the National Committee and petitioned for redress, complaining of "unlawful proceedings against her by the Court at Chickamauga."[41] However, this petition was rejected as "[t]he Committee decided they had no right to interfere with the Courts."[42]

The Pettit case has a postscript. Roughly four months later, on February 19, 1830, Principal Chief John Ross reported to Col. Montgomery, the agent for the United States, that Pettit had reconciled with his wife and was back on his former lands, making improvements. Despite the reconciliation, the principal chief considered Pettit to be an intruder and requested that he be dealt with accordingly.[43]

Thus another "safety valve" was introduced into the equation: intervention of the American government into what was once a tribal court matter. While Ross must have found it necessary to seek the help of the Americans in the case of Pettit, this type of supervisory authority remains the source of great debate today, with many tribes bristling with the thought that in exchange for increased jurisdiction (particularly to protect women from non-Indian abusers) they must first submit to greater federal court oversight.[44] A modern problem has old origins.

The collision of the American and Cherokee cultures in the early nineteenth century served to frame the Cherokees' actions within the confines of English legal tradition and for the Americans included the divergent nature of such perceived upstart behavior on the behalf of women. However, the new adjudicatory model afforded women at least some of both worlds: an opportunity to be full users, if not operators, of the Supreme Court but also continuing recourse to the old ways. Station appeared to be no obstacle. Thus, Peggy Path Killer could sue Path Killer, the principal chief himself, and obtain a judgment of $204.00 and $12.24 as the costs.[45] In this way, female participants in the system were vastly more "modern" than their contemporary American counterparts, while still maintaining a deep connection to ancient problem-solving techniques.

1. Georgia did not create a Supreme Court until 1845. History—Supreme Court of Georgia, http://www.gasupreme.us/court-information/history/.

2. This methodology is admittedly not an exact process. For one thing, the Judgment Docket contains items such as slave deeds and wills, which would only appear in local county registries, absent some case or controversy. The Cherokee percentages of female participation were based upon a "brute force," *i.e.*, hand, search of each case. Some names were not obviously male or female, including multiple Cherokee names spelled phonetically in English, and others, like "Cloud," which were simply ambiguous. I have erred on the side of seeking matches which are obvious to the twenty-first century observer. North Carolina, Tennessee, and Alabama data from 1823–1835 was distilled for each state from seven Westlaw searches:

1. plaintiff /s she (searching within full text)
2. defendant /s she (" ")
3. plaintiff /s her (" ")
4. defendant /s her (" ")
5. plaintiff /s herself (" ")
6. defendant /s herself (" ")
7. "and wife" OR "et ux." OR "et uxor" (searching only within Party field).

Searches for other gendered legal terms, *e.g.*, executrix, testatrix, etc., returned results that included their masculine/non-gendered forms, *i.e.*, executor, testator, etc., so were not used. A "brute force" search of the North Carolina Supreme Court reporter returned a slightly smaller ratio: 21.54% (249/1,156), but it nonetheless suggests a general correlation, particularly in comparison with the Cherokee cases.

3. Rosario v. Arneach, 5 Cher. Rep. 10 (2006).

4. John D. Loftin, *Constitutional Law and American Indian Religious Freedom: A Tale of Two Worlds*, 1 Am. Indian Religions 37, 38 (1994) (quoting Rennard Strickland, *American Indian Law and the Spirit World*, 1 Am. Indian L. Rev. 33 (1973)).

5. *See Id.* ("When Europeans saw nothing that seemed familiar, they concluded it simply did not exist.").

6. Carolyn Ross Johnston, Cherokee Women in Crisis: Trail of Tears, Civil War, and Allotment, 1838–1907, 146–7 (2003); *see also*, Theda Perdue, "Our Indian Heritage," *Our Mountain Heritage* (Lovin, Ed.) 39 (1979).

7. A Record Book of the Proceedings of the Supreme Court of the Cherokee Nation (unpublished document, on file with University of Tennessee Institute of Museum and Library Services) at October 29, 1827 [hereinafter Judgment Docket].

8. Judgment Docket, *supra* note 7, at October 17, 1829.

9. Perdue, *supra* note 6, at 44.

10. *Id.* at 46.

11. Theda Perdue, Cherokee Women: Gender and Culture Change, 1700 to 1835 180 (1998). To Adair, not only were the freedoms of Cherokee women incredible, he also found them unlawful. So too did early Americans: "Missionaries provide considerable evidence, however, that illicit sexual relations also took place between Cherokees. They often suspended church members—male and female—for having 'criminal intercourse.'" *Id.* Similarly, "Charles Hicks, Cherokee principal chief for a brief time before his death in 1827, was [ecclesiastically] accused and then cleared of 'criminal intercourse' with a young woman." *Id.* at 176.

12. *Id.* at 56.

13. *Id.*
14. *Id.* at 57 (citations omitted).
15. *Id.* at 56 (citations omitted).
16. *Id.* (citations omitted).
17. James Adair, The History of the American Indians 146 (1775).
18. Perdue, *supra* note 11, at 57 (citations omitted).
19. Judgment Docket, *supra* note 7, at Wednesday, October 14, 1829.
20. Cherokee Phoenix, February 4, 1829.
21. *Id.*
22. *Id.*
23. *Id.*
24. *Id.*
25. A number of notable Cherokees, including Judge John Martin, had two wives. J. Matthew Martin, *Chief Justice John Martin and the Origins of Westernized Tribal Jurisprudence*, 4 Elon L. Rev. 1, 35 (2012).
26. Laws of the Cherokee Nation 57 (spec. ed., Legal Classics Library 1995).
27. Cherokee Phoenix And Indians' Advocate (New Echota), Nov. 4, 1829.
28. *Id.*
29. *Id.*
30. *Id.*
31. Laws of the Cherokee Nation, *supra* note 26, at 142.
32. *See, e.g.*, Sharlotte Neely, Snowbird Cherokees 64–66 (1991).
33. Perdue, *supra* note 11, at 58–59.
34. Loftin, *supra* note 4, at 39.
35. *See, e.g.*, Betty Malesky, *Divorce: Dilemma for Early Americans*, (June 21, 2012), http://www.archives.com/experts/malesky-betty/divorce-in-family-history-research.html ("Absolute divorce was not legal in colonial North Carolina. A few separations were granted by the General Court with a provision for separate maintenance or alimony.").
36. Perdue, *supra* note 11, at 57–58 (citations omitted).
37. Adair, *supra* note 17, at 146.
38. Barbara Alice Mann, *Where are Your Women?: Missing in Action*, *in* Unlearning the Language of Conquest: Scholars Expose Anti-Indianism in America 123 (2006).
39. *Id.*
40. Theda Perdue, *Clan and Court, Another Look at the Early Cherokee Republic*, 24 Am. Indian Q. 562, 568 (2000).
41. Cherokee Phoenix, November 19, 1828.
42. *Id.* Limits on such a safety valve were evident for men as well. On November 1st and 4th, 1828, the National Committee took up a petition from Robert Lovett, requesting passage of a special law, granting him a new trial after the district court in Chattooga allegedly entered a judgment in his absence collecting a verdict of $60.00 from monies he had posted as a bond for the defendant, Rabbit. "After the examination of further testimony, the Committee decided that they had no power to interfere in the proceedings of the Courts, though it was evident to the house that petitioner was unjustly treated." Cherokee Phoenix, November 12, 1828.
43. Letters received by the Office of Indian Affairs, Cherokee Agency East, 1824–1881,

microformed on M-234, reel 74, at 240–43 (identifying letter of John Ross to Hugh Montgomery, February 19, 1830).

44. *See, e.g.*, Violence Against Women Reauthorization Act of 2013, Pub. L. No. 113-4, 127 Stat. 54, 56.

45. Judgment Docket, *supra* note 7, at Saturday, October 20, 1827.

Judge John Martin's grave site, Fort Gibson, OK.

5

The Court and the Institution of Slavery

The wretched state of the Cherokees, marched away from their homes at bayonet point on the Trail of Tears, remains one of the most infamous moments in the history of the United States. Often lost in the recounting of this sordid tale is the fact that struggling alongside the muddy Cherokees were people of an even lower state: the Cherokees' slaves.

Prior to contact with Europeans, the Cherokees engaged in slavery, but of a different sort than the labor market supporting colonial mercantile efforts. "Bondsmen were not important in the Cherokees' subsistence economy, and the Cherokees' lack of regard for material wealth and the absence of a profit motive contrasted sharply with European economies."[1] The Cherokee slave, "*atsi nahsa'i*," or "one who is owned," served an entirely different primary purpose; as outsiders, "anomalies," or "deviants," within the community, not quite fully human but still people, they reinforced the Cherokees' clan structure, thereby giving living proof that the "principal people" within the clans were, in fact, the "real people."[2] "Female captives among the Cherokee faced a similar range of possibilities. They could be married or adopted into clans; if these options were not available, however, they were kept as enslaved persons who labored to support their masters and existed as social outsiders."[3]

After centuries of exposure to colonial European models, and "as kinship receded in importance and as Indians began to identify with whites, Cherokees began to consider Africans to be more suitable for slavery than other Indians or Europeans."[4] However, the gentleman planter was a completely alien concept to the Cherokee, and plantation slavery, based upon the sale of commodities, developed slowly and with fits and starts as the Cherokees' transformed their traditional sexual roles, including division of labor and kinship and political systems.[5] Only then did the concept of enslavement of captives of war begin to fade from memory and the idea of racial slavery achieve normalization.[6] By the census of "1835, there were approximately" five Cherokees for every enslaved person belonging to a Cherokee in Tennessee and Alabama, twelve Cherokees per enslaved person in Georgia, "and 99 Cherokees per slave in North Carolina."[7]

Some of the Cherokees amassed substantial wealth. An "economic elite" controlled the levers of power during the Republican period prior to removal.[8] This included the judges, some of whom were prominent slaveholders.

For example, in the Coosawattee District, Judge John Martin built spectacular homes on two separate farms for his two families.[9] Both homes were magnificent for their era on the frontier and "far grander" than the homes of the average Cherokees: "The Coosawattee plantation had twenty-eight buildings (house, kitchen, smoke house, slave cabins, stables, barns, and chicken coops) and 300 acres in cultivation, plus peach and apple orchards."[10] In 1834, it produced six thousand bushels of corn and thirty-five bushels of wheat.[11] "The main dwelling was a two-story frame house, valued at four thousand dollars."[12] That the Coosawattee house was gorgeous, even a century later, seems beyond dispute: "The house is quaint and old-fashioned and beautiful. The mantel pieces have Indian carvings and the iron door hinges are of Indian workmanship.... No one can be indifferent to a spot of such natural beauty or to a body of land of such tremendous productiveness."[13] Judge Martin's wife Nellie and her eight children lived at Coosawattee.[14] Her sister Lucy, Judge Martin's other wife, and her eight children lived fifteen miles south on Salequoyah (Salacoa) Creek.[15] "The Salequoyah plantation was somewhat smaller, with only eleven buildings and 110 acres in cultivation. Between these two plantations, Martin and his wives owned eighty-nine slaves," sixty-nine stationed at the Coosawattee plantation and twenty situated at the Salacoa home.[16] His magnificent homes were made possible only by the labor of enslaved people.

Judge George M. Waters lived in a much more modest log house but owned one hundred enslaved persons.[17] His improvements at the time of the removal "included such items as seven 'negro cabins,' a smoke house, cribs, fencing, cow pens, a mill-house, and a ferry."[18]

Judge William Shorey Coodey was also a "wealthy planter."[19] Once, on the way to New Orleans, he purchased an entire family for $1,500.00: a woman and her six children, to placate his wife who did not wish to see the family separated on the auction block in New Orleans.[20]

These judges, and others, then used the new governmental structures to feather their own nests. Throughout the 1820s the National Committee and Council formalized the institution of slavery through lawmaking, and the court system became the major governmental entity charged with maintaining the Cherokees' program of human bondage.[21]

At first the laws contemplated local action, such as when the marshals were empowered to fine owners if their enslaved persons purchased and sold liquor and for the paddling of enslaved persons for the same offense.[22] By 1824, the National Council and Committee began vesting the courts with the responsibility for maintaining the slave trade.[23] Still, only a few laws regulated the trade. In the Cherokee Supreme Court, this activity was primarly presented in cases for the possession of enslaved persons (trover) or for damages for interfering with or detaining enslaved people. "The paucity of laws governing the behavior of masters and slaves in the pre-removal Cherokee slave code stands in stark contrast to the multitude of provisions of the white antebellum South."[24] Perdue suggests that the difference in the slave codes between the Cherokees and the Americans "can only be explained in terms of the enduring power of Cherokee cultural traditions."[25] Certainly the Americans and their European forebears had a head start in turning slavery into a legal institution. Nonetheless, tradition dictated that "the master continued to be responsible for the actions of his slaves just as he was for his own behavior."[26]

Some blurring occurred, with perhaps the most notorious example being that of Captain Shoe Boots, a hero of the Creek War, who, after the death of his second wife, married one of his enslaved people, Daull (or Doll[27]), and had three children with her.[28] Concerned for their precarious status as slaves, he petitioned the Council to legitimate and confer citizenship on the children (but not his wife) in 1824.[29] "The council granted the request on the condition that 'Capt. Shoe Boots cease begetting any more children by his said slave *woman*.'"[30] At the same time and with no apparent irony, he was actively engaged in the business of slavery, defending his rights to a enslaved person in the Supreme Court from the claim of a plaintiff named Water.[31] In contravention of the Council, in 1825, Shoe Boots and Daull had twins.[32] The National Committee refused to allow the emancipation of the twins.[33] Ironically, being owned by Shoe Boots' heirs may have protected them—for despite the Council's proclamation, a white man seized the three older children as slaves and only one, John Shoeboots, was able to escape and return to the Cherokee Nation and freedom.[34]

The Cherokee Supreme Court heard twenty-three matters involving slaves. While each matter in the Judgment Docket tells a story, the entries involving enslaved people tend in general to be longer, and the stories more involved.

The first slave deed recorded in the Judgment Docket came from Katy or Ka-ti Harlan, the sister of Five Killer. On October 26, 1825, she appeared before Judges Martin and Daniel and revoked any other will or power of attorney.[35] The next day she appeared and recorded a slave deed in favor of her daughter, Sarah Westall:

> To all whom these presents shall come, know that I Katy Harlan, a citizen of the Cherokee Nation, on account of the Natural Love affection which I have and feel towards my affectionate daughter Sarah Westall valued for devises other good causes & considerations use wherein, to moving do by these presents give and of my own free will record surrender up to her the said Sarah Westall my right title and claim, which I have to a Negroe woman named Quate and her two children Lose and Suse, the right of which said Negroes descended to me, as the lawful heir of my beloved brother, Five Killer.[36]

This document is strikingly similar to one proven just the previous year and found at Book 14, Page 187 of the Buncombe County, North Carolina Register of Deeds.

> Know all men by these presents that I John Webb of the State of North Carolina and County of Buncombe for valuable consideration whereof I acknowledge myself satisfied hath given and granted and by these presents do give and grant unto the said Mary Gash wife of Martin Gash said certain negro girl named Jeany about seventeen years old and her daughter Anvisy about six months old which negroes I do warrant and defend to the said Mary Gash against me and my heirs and the lawful claim of all and every person or persons.[37]

Ownership was proved in virtually the same way as the slave deeds in Buncombe County: by certification by the court.

Thus, the idea of using the court system, in particular, the Supreme Court, to prove ownership took root in the Cherokee Nation. If Katy Harlan had informally inherited her enslaved persons by intestate succession, recording the slave deed for them in the Court created a paper trail, where the chain of title might have had a break or been non-existent prior to this act. In this instance, however, the slave deed may have been more self-serving than ministerial, and Katy Harlan may have engaged in some sharp practices because the story of Quate and her children, Lose and Suse, was not over.

On Wednesday, November 1, 1826, Sarah West(all) was forced to defend her ownership rights in Quate (now referred to as "Quaity") and her two children by suing John Walker and her own mother. The nature of the suit indicates that Katy Harlan sold these individuals to John Walker. In the ensuing lawsuit, "The Court decide that Mrs. West is entitled to the negro woman Quaity only."[38] Sarah Westall then lost her rights to Quate's children, despite her mother's earlier express wishes.

If documentation were lost, recordation could prove valuable. When George Baldridge's bills of sale for Silver and Hannah were stolen, he could turn to the Court, and, with his witnesses, Charles Dry Fore Head and James Spencer, reconstruct the circumstances of their purchase.[39] With sworn testimony before Judge Adair, Baldridge filed affidavits with the Court.[40] He purchased Silver from Luther Morgan in Huntsville, Alabama, outside of the Nation.[41] This methodology, in addition to maintaining an orderly slave trade within the Nation, established a process looking outward across both state and cultural barriers, potentially protecting property from predations from Americans.

By adopting the American method of recordation, the living, breathing human element of the Cherokee slave trade became fungible across cultural boundaries. And so, on a single day in 1833, Fanny and her children, Haner, Joe, and Lily, and Patty, along with Patty's two children, Beckey and Peter, and Mary, and Jinny and her husband, Harry, and her children Sally, Charlot, George, Rosanna, Isaac, Bob, Harry, Caty, and Ellack, and her grandchildren, Reuben, Washington, Salley, and Ereline—each and every one of them—became the property of new owners.[42]

Recordation was not necessarily a sole end to a means. Litigation was another method of using the Supreme Court to resolve such matters. On Wednesday, October 25, 1826, the heirs of Bitey Springstow sued to quiet title regarding the ownership of two enslaved persons. William Burgis owned a woman named Fillis. He sold her to Bitey Springstow and Delilah McNair. Sprinsgstow then swapped Mrs. McNair a child named Darky, in exchange for all of the ownership of Fillis. However, Burgis and his wife ("the old woman Burgis") attempted to sell Fillis a second time to Delilah McNair and her husband David. The Supreme Court ruled that the Burgis' had "no right to sell her" and found for the heirs of Springstow. The Court remedied the situation by assessing damages for the loss of Fillis.[43] In this way, the Court became the final arbiter of the disputed ownership of enslaved persons in the Nation.

This process completed the reduction of Cherokee slaves to chattel property. Thus, "a negro man Simon[,] a negro woman[,] Pheby & her children" could be lumped into a suit between the administrators of the estate of Dragging Canoe and Peggy Pathkiller, along with cattle, hogs, and "one set of" blacksmithing tools.[44]

The court cases immediately involved significant money. When Mary Taylor sued Fox Taylor on Tuesday, October 18, 1825, the verdict was that Mary Taylor recover half the price the enslaved person was sold for, "say $400.00."[45] The cases were hotly contested. On November 13, 1828, the National Committee and Council determined "[t]hat the sum of fifteen dollars be, and the same is hereby appropriated out of any moneys in the National Treasury, not otherwise appropriated, for the benefit of Joshua Buffington and Alfred H. Hudson, for illegal fees collected from them, by direction of the Supreme Court in 1827."[46] Judge Martin noted that he "Rec[eived] the same costs of fifteen dollar 2nd Nov. 1829."[47]

In another example of this, Judge Martin appeared before the Supreme Court as a litigant on Thursday, October 21, 1830, in the case of *John McCarver [and] M. Gore by their agent McConnell v. John Martin*.[48] In this case, Judge Martin purchased three enslaved people from McCarver and Gore on January 1, 1830, and executed a promissory note in the "sum of three hundred and fifty dollars" as part of the consideration of the purchase.[49] When the note came due on March 1, 1830, Judge Martin refused to pay, having learned that one of the enslaved persons, an unnamed woman, was "unsound" at the time of purchase and that McCarver and Gore knew it.[50] Indeed, the Court found that the plaintiffs "purchased her as unsound property and willfully practiced a fraud by vending the same."[51] The Court then assessed damages in the sum of "only nineteen dollars and forty four and a half cents" on the debt, plus the costs.[52] McCarver and Gore attempted sharp practices on Judge Martin, but he was sharper. By using a promissory note to defer full payment, he hedged his purchase and gained valuable time to evaluate his new property.

An alternate way of understanding the value of enslaved people to the Cherokees is to consider the amount of time individuals were willing to devote to litigating over them. On Saturday, October 17, 1829, Betey (also Betsy) Walker obtained an order of attachment on three enslaved persons and sought a judgment from the Court to replevy or redeliver them to her as the rightful owner.[53]

The Court ruled in her favor.[54] A year later, on October 26, 1830, the Court entered an order that David Vann "be notified by the Clerk to be and appear personally on the first day of the term of the Supreme Court at New Echota" in 1831 to "show cause if any, why there should not be a new trial granted" in the case for "unlawfully detaining certain negroes."[55] However, the case was not heard again until Saturday, October 19, 1833, by which time the Court was meeting in Red Clay, not New Echota.[56] Thus, four years later the case finally concluded when the Court refused to grant a new trial.[57]

The use of the Court for managing the slave trade also provided a method to prove freedom.[58] On Saturday, October 25, 1834, the clerk recorded the copy of an original document in which a slave named Prince purchased his freedom and was emancipated by Caty and Annoy Richmond and Big Drum.[59]

More than just a ledger where business was recorded and rights adjudicated, the Court's actions in these cases reveal stories brimming with narratives and counter-narratives. Nowhere are these counter-narratives illustrated more vividly than in the Supreme Court filings in the matter of Chickawa.[60] Chickawa began her life as a slave named Molly in Augusta, Georgia. When she was a young girl, prior to the Revolutionary War, Molly was purchased by an Indian trader, Sam Dent.[61]

Dent had fled to Augusta to escape vengeance, the Cherokee "law of blood."[62] In the Cherokee Nation he had "by his usage of [his Cherokee wife] by beating and other wise mistreating" murdered his wife while she was pregnant.[63] The Deer Clan, "the Clan or tribe to whom she belonged determined to kill the said white man."[64] "Vengeance was a religious obligation as well as a social and judicial responsibility."[65] With his execution, the ancient law would be balanced and harmony restored. To avoid certain death if he remained in the area, Dent took a risk and purchased Molly. Following a town council meeting in the Cherokee town of Chota, Dent "did offer her to the clan [as] remuneration for the wrongs he had done."[66] This offer settled the matter, and Molly "was then and there received by [the] Deer clan and by the authorities agreeable to the Indian law and usage in the place of the murdered wife of the said Sam Dent."[67] "Molly was then emancipated and adopted into the clan composing the Deer family, agreeably to the then existing usages & customs of said Nation."[68] By operation of aboriginal law, Molly became Cherokee by virtue of her membership in the Deer clan. Her "race[,] as Europeans understood it[,] made no difference."[69] From that moment on, she was transformed and lived her life "enjoy[ing] the liberty of freedom."[70]

Molly took an Indian name, Chickawa, and later married a man named Tucker.[71] She had two sons, Edward and Isaac (who also was known as Chunestutee).[72] After the American Revolution, Chickawa and Isaac "relocated to North Carolina and took up residence among the most isolated and culturally conservative Cherokees."[73] Isaac Tucker served as one of the superintendents for the delegate election to the constitutional convention.[74] Edward, who may well have had a premonition of what was to come, emigrated to Oklahoma in 1832.[75]

In 1833, roughly sixty years after Sam Dent bargained for his life, a white woman named Molly Hightower "c[a]me into the ... Nation" and alleged that she possessed a bill of sale for Chickawa,[76] and, likely, given the circumstances, her "increase," as descendants were known, both in the trade for slaves as well as cattle. The bill of sale was from Sam Dent to Molly Hightower's father, another Indian trader.[77] Hightower's claim came at a difficult time for Chickawa and Isaac—the Cherokee government was collapsing, and what government there was now recognized a difference in skin color.[78] "In an increasingly racist Cherokee Nation, they had African ancestry, and the waning importance of clan ties, which had defined mother and sons as Cherokees, left them vulnerable."[79]

The Deer clan rose to defend Chickawa, the former slave.[80] In addition to Chickawa and Isaac Tucker, prominent members of the Deer Clan from North Carolina signed a petition on her behalf, and on that of Isaac. The Doctor, Chis nes Tustee Adasi, Charles Buffington, The Old, Bucks Horn, and Chicked Indian Man all averred to the adoption of Molly and to her transformation into Chickawa.[81] With this petition in hand, Isaac Tucker made his way from North Carolina to Red Clay, Tennessee, where he met up with more of his kin from the Deer clan and they proceeded to the courthouse.

Together, they appeared before Judge Daniel McCoy, who put Big Half Breed, White Path, John Watts, and Tiger under oath, and they executed an affidavit, bootstrapping the North Carolina statement as an exhibit. There they created a court record. Charles Vann, the clerk, gave the originals back to Isaac Tucker, once it had been transcribed into the Judgment Docket.

When Molly was adopted into the Deer Clan some sixty years earlier, no such legal niceties existed. Dent could have executed a manumission document of some sort, but he was, no doubt, just grateful to escape with his hide intact. In any event, there was nowhere to file it at the time. Furthermore, Dent wasn't participating in a commercial slavery transaction: his life was deeply involved in a matter of ancient, tribal customs and traditions: the bedrock of indigenous law. Molly was not deeded as property; rather she was transformed into a

Cherokee person. Any commercialization of the circumstances would probably have only perplexed the community gathered at Chota when the bargain was struck. It is likely that only later, when he had a moment to reflect on the event, did Dent realize no title had changed hands, and he could make a fee by selling Molly to Hightower's father.

Historians have consistently misunderstood what occurred before Judge McCoy. McLoughlin wrote that "the case came before the Cherokee Supreme Court" and that the Court "ruled" in Chickawa's favor.[82] It did not. He then concludes that "[t]he agents of Molly Hightower had to return to Georgia without" Chickawa or Isaac. Nothing in the Judgment Docket supports this. Perdue confuses the statement written in North Carolina with an affidavit and misconstrues the actual affidavit acknowledged by Judge McCoy as a decision, writing "the court recognized the legitimacy of the claim and granted national protection to the Tuckers."[83] Lowery makes a similar error, finding that the Court "sided" with the Deer clan.[84] Instead, the Judgment Docket reveals the Court took no action: this was a recordation only. The bootstrapping should be instantly familiar to modern lawyers and judges. It is still resorted to on occasion as a method to tack an inadmissible document onto one that might be received by the court into evidence.

Despite being incorrect from a legal perspective, Perdue's ultimate thesis seems cogent. "The experience of Chickawa and Isaac demonstrates that Cherokees not only recognized the importance of clans and matrilineal kin ties but they also used political innovations to confirm traditional social relations and values."[85] This understanding leads to the conclusion "that two legal systems," one ancient and aboriginal, and one modern and Western, "operated simultaneously in the early Cherokee republic."[86]

Just as in the modern Hopi court system, the very existence of the tribal court system in the 1830s and the resource of formal tribal law, as opposed to custom and culture, was, in this example, "constituted by [Cherokee] legal actors through narrative interactions that allowe[ed] the articulation of both Anglo-style notions of legal process and [Cherokee] notions of tradition."[87] These interactions constitute a co-narration of the story of Chickawa, both legally, in a way understood in the slave trade, while, at the same time, informing it with "'truths' grounded in 'relational' notions of [Cherokee] tradition that are 'outside' Anglo-style law."[88] This co-narrative is "constituted through negotiations between an Anglo-style narrative coherence ... and the juridical accommodation of [the Deer clan's] desire for a tradition-based legal rationale that works 'outside' the Anglo-style truth making of the court."[89]

This co-narration of "law," both ancient and modern, is what troubles the Supreme Court so greatly today. Its antecedents can clearly be seen in the story of the enslaved child Molly, who became the Cherokee woman named Chickawa.

1. Theda Perdue, Slavery and the Evolution of Cherokee Society 1540–1866 18 (1979).

2. *Id.* at 4, 17–18. Some generalities applied across "historical and ancient cultures." "A society's captives rarely attained equal status with the native born. When warriors returned, those captives destined to be slaves almost always underwent a process that sociologist Orlando Patterson of Harvard University calls 'social death,' in which they were stripped of their natal identity and 'reborn' as slaves." Catherine M. Cameron, *How Captives Changed the World*, Sci. Am., Dec. 2017, at 79–80.

3. Terri L. Snyder, *Women, Race and the Law*, Oxford Res. Encyclopedia of Am. Hist. (September 2015), http://americanhistory.oxfordre.com/view/10.1093/acrefore/9780199329175.001.0001/acrefore-9780199329175-e-12.

4. Perdue, *supra* note 1, at 49.

5. *Id.* at 50.

6. Tiya Miles, The House on Diamond Hill 59 (2010).

7. Perdue, *supra* note 1, at 166 n. 2.

8. *Id.* at 56.

9. Elizabeth Arnett Fields, *Between Two Cultures: Judge John Martin and the Struggle for Cherokee Sovereignty*, *in* The S. Colonial Backcountry: Interdisc. Persp. on Frontier Communities 191 (D. Crass et al. eds., Univ. of Tenn. Press, 1998); Patricia Lockwood, *Judge John Martin*, 64 Chron. of Okla. 61, 64 (1986).

10. Fields, *supra* note 9, at 191.

11. *Id.*

12. *Id.*

13. Lola Selmon Beeson, *Homes of Distinguished Cherokee Indians*, 11 Chron. of Okla. 933 (1933). Beeson may be confusing the George Harlan house, known for many years as "Carter's Quarters" or "Rock Spring" with Judge Martin's house. Recent scholarship suggests that, while the two houses were "very similar," Judge Martin's house was actually at the Coosawattee River. Robert S. Davis, Jr., *But Where Was the John Martin House?*, In the Shadow of the Mountains 50–51(2003). This seems more likely. Unfortunately, the John Martin house fell into disrepair and was purchased in 1970 by the Army Corps of Engineers who demolished it as part of the Carter's Dam project. *Id.* at 50.

14. Fields, *supra* note 9, at 191.

15. *Id.*

16. Lockwood, *supra* note 9, at 66.

17. Perdue, *supra* note 1, at 58–9.

18. *Id.* at 59.

19. *Id.* at 92.

20. *Id.* at 108.

21. Prior to the creation of the Tribal court system, the Committee and National Council adjudicated matters themselves. *See, e.g.*, Laws of the Cherokee Nation 8–9 (spec. ed., Legal Classics Library 1995) In the case of a runaway belonging to William Thompson who sold a stolen horse to Otter Lifter, the National Council found no liability in Thompson and abrogated any contract or bargain entered into by a slave without the approval of the master. Miles argues that this stands for the proposition "that slaves acquired property and entered into contracts, but it also assigned a degree of autonomy to slaves in their business dealings." Miles, *supra* note 6 at 92 (2010). This misreads the case. The Council was holding

that, absent any agreement from the master, any purported contracts or bargains on the part of a slave were void.

22. Laws of the Cherokee Nation, *supra* note 21, at 24.

23. *See, e.g.*, Laws of the Cherokee Nation, *supra* note 21, at 34 (employing slaves of United States citizens without a permit); 38 (miscegenation criminalized).

24. Perdue, *supra* note 1, at 57.

25. *Id.* at 58

26. *Id.*

27. Miles, *supra* note 6, at 148.

28. William G. McLoughlin, Cherokee Renascence in the New Republic 345 (1986).

29. *Id.*; *see also* Perdue, *supra* note 1, at 84.

30. Perdue, *supra* note 1, at 84–85.

31. A Record Book of the Proceedings of the Supreme Court of the Cherokee Nation (unpublished document, on file with University of Tennessee Institute of Museum and Library Services) at Friday, October 29, 1824 [hereinafter Judgment Docket].

32. McLoughlin, *supra* note 28, at 345.

33. *Id.*

34. *Id.*

35. Judgment Docket, *supra* note 31, at Wednesday, October 26, 1825.

36. Judgment Docket, *supra* note 31, at Thursday, October 27, 1825.

37. Buncombe County, Register of Deeds: Slave Deeds, https://www.buncombecounty.org/governing/depts/register-of-deeds/slave-deeds/default.aspx.

38. Judgment Docket, *supra* note 31, at Wednesday, November 1, 1826.

39. Judgment Docket, *supra* note 31, at Monday, September 27, 1830.

40. *Id.*

41. *Id.*

42. *See* Judgment Docket, *supra* note 31, at Thursday, October 24, 1833. Jinny's family stayed within the family of their previous owners, the Vanns, as Mary Stedman sold them to her brother. Miles, *supra* note 6, at 224–25. Miles spells Jinny's name as "Jenny," Harry's as "Jarry," Rosanna's as "Roseanna," and Charlot's as "Charlat." *Id.*

43. Judgment Docket, *supra* note 31, at Wednesday, October 25, 1826.

44. Judgment Docket, *supra* note 31, at Tuesday, November 4, 1828.

45. Judgment Docket, *supra* note 31, at Tuesday, October 18, 1825.

46. Laws of the Cherokee Nation, *supra* note 21, at 108; *see also* Judgment Docket, *supra* note 31, at Wednesday, October 17, 1827.

47. Judgment Docket, *supra* note 31, at Wednesday, October 17, 1827.

48. Judgment Docket, *supra* note 31, at Thursday, October 21, 1830.

49. *Id.*

50. *Id.*

51. *Id.*

52. *Id.*

53. Judgment Docket, *supra* note 31, at Saturday, October 17, 1829.

54. *Id.*

55. Judgment Docket, *supra* note 31, at Tuesday, October 26, 1830.

56. *See, e.g.*, Judgment Docket, *supra* note 31, at Friday, October 18, 1833.

57. Judgment Docket, *supra* note 31, at Saturday, October 19, 1833.

58. "No law was ever passed regulating the manumission of slaves by Cherokee owners." McLoughlin, *supra* note 28, at 341.

59. Judgment Docket, *supra* note 31, at Saturday, October 25, 1834.

60. Chickawa's name is also spelled Chickaw in the Judgment Docket. Scholars have generally spelled it Chickaw, although McLaughlin spells it Chichkaune.

61. Theda Perdue, *Clan and Court: Another Look at the Early Cherokee Republic*, 24 Am. Indian Q., No. 4, 562 (2000).

62. For an excellent discussion of aboriginal Cherokee legal constructs, *see* John Phillip Reid, A Law of Blood: The Primitive Law of the Cherokee Nation (1970).

63. Judgment Docket, *supra* note 31, at Friday, October 18, 1833.

64. *Id.*

65. Perdue, *supra* note 61, at 563.

66. Judgment Docket, *supra* note 31, at Friday, October 18, 1833.

67. *Id.*

68. *Id.*

69. Perdue, *supra* note 61, at 563.

70. Judgment Docket, *supra* note 31, at Friday, October 18, 1833.

71. Perdue, *supra* note 61, at 563.

72. *Id.*

73. *Id.* at 564.

74. Laws of the Cherokee Nation, *supra* note 21, at 76.

75. Perdue, *supra* note 61, at 565.

76. Judgment Docket, *supra* note 31, Friday, October 18, 1833. McLaughlin suggests that Hightower herself did not venture into the Cherokee Nation, but rather sent surrogates, agents, early "slave catchers," who acted as a proxy in exchange for fees when the re-enslaved person was delivered to the putative owner. McLoughlin, *supra* note 28, at 347; *see also, e.g.*, Cherokee Phoenix, June 12, 1830 ("We are told three Georgia officers were the other day about Hightower, hunting some negroes, belonging to Shoe Boot's estate, but they were obliged to return without a booty. A forged deed of gift is the foundation of the claim.").

77. McLoughlin, *supra* note 28, at 347.

78. Perdue, *supra* note 61, at 565.

79. *Id.*

80. *Id.* at 567.

81. Judgment Docket, *supra* note 31, at Friday, October 18, 1833.

82. McLoughlin, *supra* note 28, at 347.

83. Perdue, *supra* note 61, at 567–68.

84. Malinda Lowery, *Cherokee Law of Blood,* National History Education Clearinghouse http://teachinghistory.org/best-practices/examples-of-historical-thinking/23417.

85. Perdue, *supra* note 61, at 568.

86. *Id.*

87. Justin B. Richland, Arguing with Tradition 24 (2008).

88. *Id.* at 25.

89. *Id.* at 120.

Principal Chief John Ross, from his monument on the square in Tahlequah, OK.

6

The Criminal Jurisprudence of the Court

The nature of criminal prosecution in the original Cherokee courts was different in some ways from the familiar, modern context. For one, "[g]rand juries and tribal prosecution by an official solicitor were not introduced into the Cherokee legal system until after the Civil War. Until that time criminal indictment was essentially a private procedure instituted by a wronged individual."[1] Prosecutors do appear in the record as appointed counsel, and were required to post a bond for their services.[2] Punishments included "confiscation, fines," and "corporeal punishment," including flogging, "ear cropping and death," typically by hanging.[3]

In these new laws, however, there were many rights and protections instantly familiar to modern Americans: a due process right, a right to a remedy at law, a right of confrontation, a right to speedy and public trial, a right to trial by jury, a right to bail, a right to have compulsory process, a prohibition of compulsory self-incrimination, a prohibition of unreasonable searches and seizures, a prohibition of general warrants, and a prohibition of double jeopardy.[4]

An additional protection for the accused included trial by indictment.[5] Under Article V, Section 11 of the Cherokee Constitution of 1827, indictments were to "run in the name of the Cherokee Nation."[6] Indictments were to include allegations of the date, defendant, and crime.[7] Additionally, indictments included constitutionally compulsory, conclusory language that the alleged crime was "against the peace and dignity" of the Nation.[8]

Article V, Section 8 of the 1827 Constitution provided that "[t]he Judges of the Supreme Court and Circuit Courts shall have comple[te] criminal Jurisdiction in such cases and in such manner as may be pointed out by law."[9] Although no Supreme Court cases divulge the prosecution of Americans before it, the evidence suggests that the lower courts did, on occasion, exercise criminal jurisdiction over citizens of the Unites States. Scholars should not underestimate the significance of these events. Careful analysis of the exercise of criminal jurisdiction by the Cherokee Supreme Court and lower courts from 1823 to 1835 demonstrates the extent of those courts' retained primeval power and clearly shows that such authority is the equivalent of Chief Justice Marshall's "actual state of things."[10] As evidenced by its operation of its own judicial systems, as well as by approving actions of agents of the United States, the Cherokee Nation's exercise of criminal jurisdiction during the existence of its original Supreme Court remained consistent with the Cherokees' dependent status. Prior to removal, the Cherokee courts exercised full criminal jurisdiction historically consistent with the dependent status of the Cherokee court system.

After July of 1827, crimes alleged to have been committed within the Cherokee Nation were defined constitutionally and can be recognized by their own lawful definitions.[11] They are clearly labeled with the Cherokee Nation as the plaintiff.[12] However, between 1823 and 1827, identification is slightly more problematic because the Judgment Docket is a little oblique in certain cases as to whether the case is a crime or a tort.[13]

For example, it might be tempting to label *James Foster v. Jesse Vann*, by his administrator, as the first criminal case to come before the Cherokee Supreme Court on October 16, 1823, "for a crime of grand larceny."[14] But such a conclusion would lead to a quirk: a criminal action apparently not abating with the death of the offender and thus being prosecuted against his estate in the manner of a bill of attainder.[15] However, this case resulted in an action that has to charm the modern practitioner: it was continued.[16]

The case returned to the docket four years later, on Monday, October 29, 1827, with a slightly different caption: *James Foster v. The Peacock, Exec. of Jesse Vann, Decd.*[17] Here we learn that the case was actually for "[r]ecovery of stolen cattle."[18] Since by this time criminal cases were clearly running in the name of the Nation, this case is actually a civil claim upon a decedent's estate.[19]

In comparing the Cherokee Supreme Court cases with cases from the neighboring state supreme courts, those courts' criminal cases will appear more familiar to the modern reader simply because the protection of the grand jury was hardwired into the state constitutions from the outset.[20] Furthermore, like today, many crimes against the state may also be torts, for which private individuals may bring civil actions. In this analysis each entry regarding a matter before the Cherokee Supreme Court, particularly those prior to the enactment of the Constitution of 1827, required examination to determine whether the facts disclose the elements of a crime or the punishment of one, even if the subject matter of the case appears to be a private wrong, such as "pleas of defraud" or hog stealing.[21]

The criminal cases account for 9.5% of the total number of matters and 11.2% of the actual cases and controversies. In eleven of the twenty-four criminal appeals heard by the Cherokee Supreme Court, no charge is specified other than a usual, but not completely consistent, notation: "breaking" or "violating the Cherokee Law."[22] These otherwise undistinguished cases nevertheless offer glimpses into the processes of the Cherokee Supreme Court.

The first criminal appeal taken up by the Cherokee Supreme Court was *Cherokee Nation v. Elisha Dyer*, heard on November 1, 1824.[23] In this case, the Supreme Court found "no bill" and apparently dismissed the case.[24] The Court clearly determined that it had the authority to look into the sufficiency of the charges and to adjudicate accordingly.[25] Similarly, on October 26, 1825, in *Thomas Fields v. Cyrus Blanks*, on a charge of "violation of the Cherokee Law," the Court found "no bill."[26] Finally, in the first murder case the Court adjudicated, *Cherokee Nation v. Gah Co We*, an "indictment for murder of Ezthral Wright, Kingstick's brother, we the judges of the supreme court find no bill against the dft Gah Co We."[27] The Court did not hesitate to dismiss a case, even one as serious as murder, if it concluded that the foundational charging document was insufficient.[28]

The Cherokee Supreme Court did not hesitate to dismiss other criminal cases as well, displaying somewhat of a reluctance to show any favoritism for the new republic.[29] For example, despite the hazards of frontier travel, and the indisputable fact that the Court itself had been continued on more than one occasion when judges were missing, the Court was swift to dismiss the case of *Cherokee Nation v. Edward Crittinton Taluskee*, on October 28, 1826, when "no prosecutor" was present.[30] No judge rose to intercede on behalf of the nation.[31] Modern practitioners of criminal defense might find such judicial restraint refreshing. Incidents like this may have led to the November 8, 1828, passage of a law requiring prosecutors to post a bond:

> Whereas, much inconcenience is experienced by the courts in this Nation, in the trial of criminal cases, in consequences of prosecutors not being bound for the prosecution of such criminal cases, therefore,
>
> Resolved by the Committee and Council, in General Council convened, That after the passage of this act, any person or persons, not a public officer, who shall undertake to prosecute any criminal or criminals shall be, and he, she, or they are hereby required to give bond and security, in a sum double the amount of such prosecution,

> for the faithful performance of prosecuting the criminals, who may be arrested and brought to trial.
>
> Be it further resolved by the authorities aforesaid, That it shall be the duty of such prosecutors to give bond and security previous to their receiving warrants for the arresting of such criminals.[32]

Other undocumented, alleged crimes illustrate the fact that the Court served as a *de novo* tribunal, not merely as a court of appeals and errors.[33] On October 24, 1825, John Miller was acquitted by the Court of "violating the Cherokee Law."[34] The next day, the case of *Archy Foreman v. William Blyth* came on for trial before a jury.[35] The case spilled over into the following day, at which time "the jury found that he did not violate the Cherokee Law."[36] This power to try criminal cases *de novo* was recognized in law on October 18, 1828, when the National Council enacted a statute providing, among other things, that:

> the Supreme Judges elected agreeably to the Constitution, shall compose the Supreme Court, and shall have full power to try, and decide all cases upon the Supreme Court docket, that remain untried, which may come under the jurisdiction of the laws of the Nation, and shall have complete cognizance of all cases appealed from the several circuit Courts, as may be pointed out by law. The Supreme Court shall also have power to act and decide upon criminal cases without reference to appeals from the Circuit Courts.[37]

An appeal to the Supreme Court thus offered litigants not only a second bite at the apple, but also the possibility of a completely different jury pool; these appellate cases were heard in New Echota (in what is now north Georgia) and were often far removed from their original venues.[38]

We do not know and we cannot tell from the Judgment Docket what processes triggered the opportunity for a jury trial *de novo*.[39] In 1825 in *Thomas Fields v. John Miller*, the Court decided the case without input from the jury, holding: "[i]t is the opinion of the Court that the defendant be fined $5.00" for this violation of the Cherokee Law.[40] Similarly, in *Cherokee Nation v. Brice Martin* the "Court found for defendant" without referring the matter to the jury.[41] Likewise, the Court found the defendant guilty in the case of *Cherokee Nation v. Jesse Ratley*.[42] The Court minute book indicates that Ratley was a prisoner.[43] There was no national prison; instead, defendants were kept under guard.[44] Upon finding himself under guard at the time he came before the Court, Ratley perhaps sought an expeditious disposition in a bench trial rather than awaiting the arrival of the jurors. In *Archey Foreman for Cherokee Nation v. William M.J. Evnkize*, a finding for the defense left no culpable party to pay the $9.75 witness fee for twelve days of inconvenience on the part of Major Martin.[45] It is unclear whether the exonerated defendant was required to pay the witness fee nonetheless.

A finding of guilt was not specifically rendered for a particular "felony" [sic] in *Cherokee Nation v. John Fields,* where the clerk noted that "[t]he Court decide that the defendant pay to the Nation three dollars, considered to be the per Cent due, & two dollars to the plaintiff for damages."[46] Likewise, in another case "for breaking the Cherokee Law," *Archie Foreman v. Richard Huffacre,* the clerk noted that the defendant confessed judgment in the sum of ten dollars and that the Court awarded the costs of the lawsuit in the amount of $4.50.[47] These two cases show that the Court dipped into its reservoir of equitable powers in assessing restitution and approving the defendant's admitted amount of damages.[48]

"Horse theft thus appears to have been the most common crime in the first quarter of the 19th Century and the most difficult to restrain among the Cherokees and whites."[49] "More enforcement machinery [was] directed [towards it] than any other one crime."[50] The crime grew to include more than the theft of horses: enterprising criminals began a brisk business in selling stolen livestock.[51]

The *Cherokee Phoenix* reprinted an article from the *Southern Advocate* which described how horse theft had morphed into organized crime:

> Pony Club in Carroll County, Georgia.- We are informed by a gentleman who has recently passed through that place, of indubitable credibility, that there is a CLUB, who make a profession of stealing horses as well from their own citizens as from strangers. Their plans, from their contiguity and intercourse with the Cherokees, have been so judiciously executed as to elude detection. They do not we understand, profess to take the life of a traveller, but only his horse, in order, it may be presumed, that in cases of conviction, their punctilious clemency may establish a contested principle in penal law, that there is a distinct and tangible difference in value between property and life. This policy reminds us of the reply of Judge Burnet, to the horse-stealer, who upon being asked what he had to say, why judgment of death should not be passed upon him, and answering, "that it was hard to hang a man for only stealing a horse," was told by the Judge, 'Man, thou art not only to be hanged for stealing a horse, but that horses may not be stolen.' That punishments should be proportioned to offences [sic] is just and politic we admit, but that there is a lamentable deficiency in the justice and morality of this new country overlooking the *alieni appetens* which is so manifestly a nuisance to their neighbors and strangers, is equally notorious.

> We have frequently heard of this pony club.—It is said by a Traveller who passed this place some time since directly from Carroll, that this stealing association has become so dexterious [sic] in its profession, that if the d___l had been in the shape of a pony, he would ere this have fallen a prey to its agility. "Pony club" is but a limited name and will by no means give a correct idea of this neighboring combination—"cow club," "hog club," &c. may properly be added.[52]

The "Pony Club" continued to plague the Cherokee Nation throughout the late 1820s:

> Another racer gone to the Poney [sic] Club Carroll County, Georgia, or to some other place of similar distinction. On Tuesday or Wednesday last was taken without my leave, a small dark chesnut [sic] sorrel Mare, blazed face, all feet white, her fore legs white nearly to the knees, bare-footed all round, and rather wild when handled by a stranger particularly and mane very short, owing to her having the Lampers.
>
> There is some reason to suspect a lurking kind of white man, who left this place about that time on his way to Marion Co. Ten. or Jackson Co. Alabama. Friends to the suppression of such villainy, are earnestly requested in all the adjacent states, to keep a sharp look out. I will give ten dollars for the delivery of the thief & mare to me at this place, or five for the mare alone if caught in the Nation.
>
> ISAAC H. HARRIS.
> Nov. 5th, 1828[53]

The existence of organized crime made it a relatively simple matter to use the criminal racket for political purposes as well.[54] The "Pony Club" was suggested to be at the forefront of a wave of intruders into the nation who, "[i]nstead of stealing," began to shoot the horses and cattle of the Cherokees.[55] Theft or destruction of horses, the main method of transport across the vast distances of the Cherokee Nation, affected commerce, communication and travel.[56] The destruction of cattle eliminated food stores.[57]

The failure of the United States government to protect the boundaries of the Indian Nation forced the National Council to take action, even though the Cherokees had not expelled intruders on a large scale before:

> [o]ne group of about twenty families, members of a gang of horse thieves called the Pony Club, had squatted along the main road to Alabama, and the Council was afraid that the Cherokees would be blamed for their

crimes. The Council appointed Major Ridge, a prominent figure with a distinguished record as war leader and public servant, to lead a troop of Light Horse, the national police force, to evict the intruders. They did so, burning out the families, who later testified that they were terrified by Ridge, who wore a buffalo skull headdress complete with horns, and his men, painted for war. A posse from Carroll County tracked the Cherokee Light Horse and captured four, one of whom they beat to death. The others they carried off to jail. On the way, two escaped, but the third, Rattling Gourd, they held. Hugh Montgomery, the federal agent assigned to the Cherokee Nation, got him released with the argument that he was not an officer in the Light Horse, made no decisions, and was simply following orders. The central question, the right of the sheriff of Carroll County, Georgia, to enter the Cherokee Nation and arrest four Cherokees (not to mention killing one of them) for acting in accordance with a treaty provision, remained unanswered.[58]

With no answer to the central question of the competing attempts by Georgia to exercise criminal jurisdiction within the Cherokee Nation, the issues were destined to repeat themselves.[59] The varieties were almost without limit.[60] In 1827, a Cherokee citizen named Old Man was charged in Carroll County, Georgia, with the murder of a citizen of Georgia, one Dennis May.[61] Old Man was arrested by Georgia authorities, but while crossing the Chatahoochee River, he dove in the water and escaped in the darkness.[62] Believing the fugitive to have fled to the Cherokee Nation, the governor of Georgia demanded that Indian Agent Hugh Montgomery assist in the extradition.[63] The Cherokees responded to Montgomery that they would assist in locating and apprehending Old Man, but insisted that he be tried in the United States District Court as provided, for example, by Article VI of the Treaty of Hopewell, November 28, 1785.[64] Fulminating, the governor of Georgia dashed off a curt reply to Montgomery on December 12, 1827:

> The place where, and the court, by whom he will be tried are matters to be settled, here, in settling these questions we shall not consult Mr. Hicks or pay any respect either to his wishes or opinions. You will no doubt conceive it to be your duty, however, to instruct the Cherokees that Justice will be done and a fair trial had, whether the State[']s Judges or the United States Judges preside at it.[65]

Several times Georgia and Tennessee exercised criminal jurisdiction over Cherokee Indians for crimes allegedly occurring within the Cherokee Nation.[66] Indeed, this was the basis for Georgia's notorious challenge to the supremacy of the United States Constitution through the State's infamous lynching of George Tassell, hung by the State before the Supreme Court of the United States could hear his plea.[67]

Georgia did not limit itself to asserting jurisdiction over the Cherokees—it attempted to assert criminal jurisdiction over United States soldiers operating in the Cherokee Nation under orders of the federal government.[68] On October 14, 1824, James Williams wrote the Secretary of War to report on his actions, along with Col. Archibald Turk's company, in removing intruders from Cherokee lands.[69] In particular, he enclosed a Bill of Indictment from Hall County, Georgia, in which he, Col. Turk, and others were indicted on August 11, 1824, for the murder of James Dickson, an illegal white settler in Cherokee Nation lands "not having the fear of God before their eyes, but being moved and instigated by the devil."[70] On January 6, 1825, Col. Turk wrote the Secretary, requesting his assistance for the upcoming trial.[71]

While Georgia sought to exercise jurisdiction over Cherokees, one case documents the Cherokee Nation's judicial branch of government exercising criminal jurisdiction over a white citizen of Georgia.[72] On September 19, 1829, Jesse Stancell, a "white man," was arrested within the Cherokee Nation at Elejay and charged with horse stealing.[73] Stancell was detained "in close custody for the space of thirty hours" during which time he was tried by a jury.[74] George Saunders, who the Judgment Docket reveals had previously served as foreman of Cherokee Supreme Court juries, served in the same capacity on Stancell's jury.[75] Stancell was sentenced "to receive fifty stripes on the bare back, which was fifty less than what [was] common ... for such offence."[76] His captors "stripped [him], tied [him] up to a tree" and executed the sentence upon him.[77] Saunders averred that "[w]e acted agreeably to the laws of our country in punishing the man."[78]

Crossing back into Georgia following this indignity, Stancell immediately made his way to the chambers of the Honorable Augustin S. Clayton, "Judge of the Supreme Courts of the western Circuit of" the State of Georgia and judicial nemesis of the Cherokees.[79] Stancell's affidavit before Judge Clayton omitted the stolen horse and his jury trial.[80] The affidavit characterized him not as a thief, but as a victim "to the great effusion of his blood, the laceration of his back and sides, leaving deep wounds, gashes and bruises on the same."[81]

Judge Clayton issued criminal process for the arrest of Saunders, who reported to the *Phoenix* as follows:

> [t]he officers of that state sent armed men to take all the Indians that were concerned in whipping him. I understood that they were on their way, and went to the Long Swamp to meet them. They met me there.

I there gave them my bond and security for my appearance at court at Gainsville in Hall County.[82]

The case continued to simmer for the next year. In his annual message to the people on October 16, 1830, Principal Chief John Ross commented on "the case of Judge Sanders for punishing a whiteman [sic] under the laws of the nation, for the crime of horse stealing" in a litany of complaints against the Georgia judiciary in general and Judge Clayton in particular.[83] Among other actions, Georgia responded by passing a statute in 1830 which provided in part:

Sec. 3. And be it further enacted by the authority aforesaid. That after the time aforesaid, it shall not be lawful for any person or persons, under colour, or by authority, of the Cherokee tribe, or any of its laws or regulations, to hold any court or tribunal whatever, for the purpose of hearing and determining causes, civil or criminal; or to give any judgment in such causes, or to issue, or cause to issue any process against the person or property of any of said tribe. And all persons offending against the provisions of this section, shall be guilty of a high misdemeanor, and subject to indictment, and on conviction thereof shall be imprisoned in the penitentiary at hard labour for the space of four years.[84]

This example exposes the exercise of criminal jurisdiction over a citizen of the United States by the tribal court.[85] Such action is seen to be in the continuum of push and pull on the frontier between the states and the Cherokee Nation, with the Nation seeking a successful mechanism of enforcement of law in order to maintain stability.[86] In this context, the Nation's exercise of enforcement machinery is both understandable and legitimate; it also reflected the actual state of affairs.

Despite the ravings of Georgians, the Cherokee Nation prosecuted Cherokee Indians for horse theft in the tribal courts.[87] In the first Cherokee Supreme Court case specifically denominated as horse theft, David Quinton, Sr. was acquitted on Saturday, October 21, 1826.[88] On Wednesday, May 21, 1828, the *Phoenix* reported on a trial of Cherokees who were convicted of stealing horses from whites in neighboring Carroll County, Georgia:

At the last Circuit Court held in Hightower, three persons were convicted for stealing horses out of Carrol [sic] Co. & were sentenced to receive fifty lashes each. These persons, we are told, stole upon the principle of rendering evil for evil. How backward some of our neighboring whites may be to do justice to the Indians, *we confess we feel a pleasure in noticing this instance of the impartiality of our courts.* It would be well if the authorities of Carrol [sic] County (Gov. Forsythe's [sic] Ministers) will look about and punish their offending citizens. It would be a sweeping work if they were to begin. So much "for the success of the new Constitution."[89]

It is possible that one of those three persons tried in Hightower, John C. Bird, appealed to the Cherokee Supreme Court. On October 28, 1828, in *The Nation v. John C. Bird*, the defendant entered a guilty plea to horse stealing and was sentenced to receive 100 lashes, fifty more than the number imposed at the circuit court level earlier that year.[90]

Other theft crimes occupied significant portions of the Cherokee Supreme Court's docket.[91] Friday, October 24, 1828, saw two cases of alleged stealing.[92] In *Cherokee Nation v. Robert Saunders & Wayahuttah*, the defendants were acquitted of stealing money, despite the efforts of a prosecutor named Wolf.[93] In the next case, Beaver Carrier was convicted of theft and sentenced to receive seventy five lashes.[94] In 1827, Bledsoe Gore was acquitted of theft.[95] The final criminal case heard by the Cherokee Supreme Court was a multi-defendant jury trial for hog stealing.[96] In a mixed verdict the six-man jury found Choo Noo Las Kee guilty and fined him $10.00, but acquitted Rain Crow and Sleeping Rabbit.[97]

The dockets of the lower courts also exhibit multiple cases of theft: "We understand that two thieves were lately tried at Coosewaytee. One was a very noted one, whose name we have the honor of publishing in our paper. Both were found guilty. The principal one received one hundred lashes on the bare back, and the other fifty."[98]

Murder was the most serious crime to come before the Cherokee Supreme Court. Willful murder in the Cherokee Nation was punishable by death.[99] Three documented murder cases came before the Cherokee Supreme Court during its existence.[100] None of the three cases resulted in a conviction before the Court.[101] As noted above, in the first murder case, the Court found the indictment to be defective.[102] In the third murder case, a twelve-person jury found The Broom not guilty on Wednesday, October 29, 1834.[103]

The second murder case reviewed by the Supreme Court, *Cherokee Nation v. Noo Cha Wee*, is intriguing in that it anticipates the frantic efforts of modern capital trial counsel to litigate on multiple fronts at the last minute.[104] It also demonstrates an assumption of criminal jurisdiction by the legislative and executive branches, problems that continue to plague tribal courts to this day.[105]

The case was heard by the Court on October 19, 1829, and reported on October 21, 1829.[106] Noo Cha Wee, "a criminal, who had been condemned to die on that day by the circuit court of Aquohee District for the murder of Ahmahyouhah," requested that the sentence imposed be suspended.[107] After some deliberation, marked in the Judgment Docket by the scratching out of preliminary rulings, the Court held: "The sentence having been [im]posed in the Circuit Court, this Court decide that they have no power of suspending the sentence of said Circuit Court."[108] Here we find an example of the Court declining criminal jurisdiction, which might affect the sentence in a homicide case.[109] The decision is notable for its deference to the authority of the lower court, recognizing the appellate court's proper role reviewing errors or trying cases where it had original jurisdiction.[110] In this declination, the Court foreshadowed the trend of modern courts to avoid re-litigating homicide cases.[111]

Noo Cha Wee and his supporters were not quite finished, though. Moving swiftly, at two o'clock that afternoon, the day of his scheduled execution, Noo Cha Wee appeared before the clerk of the National Council with a petition containing "upwards of fifty signatures, praying" for a reprieve of his death sentence.[112] The National Committee immediately took the matter up and considered a special law, "repriev[ing] and discharg[ing him] from the sentence of death that was pronounced against him by the Circuit Judge, Daniel M'Coy."[113]

> [a]fter short addresses, the question was put, shall the prisoner be reprieved of [sic] not?—yeas 31 Nays.3 A resolution for the reprieve of the prisoner was then drawn and signed and sent to the principal Chief for his approval. He being absent, the Assistant principal Chief put his signature to the instrument. The prisoner was then set at liberty.[114]

Indeed, "the Council felt compelled to place him 'under the protection of the laws of this Nation,' presumably because the victim's relatives presented a genuine threat to his life."[115]

In this instance, the National Council stepped in where the Court would not.[116] The *Cherokee Phoenix* explained the extenuating circumstances: "It appeared from the evidence by which he was convicted that the murder was not premeditated or willful. The criminal did the fatal deed under mitigating circumstances."[117] The restraint of the Court, then, resulted in the National Council assuming jurisdiction to consider evidence of the crime, which is a judicial function.[118] However, the attestation of George Lowrey, the assistant principal chief, actually makes this action function exactly as a pardon.

The lack of murder convictions in the Supreme Court does not indicate that the crime was taken lightly, however. Multiple defendants were hung for the crime. But no one was executed in the name of the national government until 1827, and that defendant was a Creek.[119]

Ardent spirits were also asserted as causation for "a murder ... committed not far from Crutchfield's mill, by one O-lah [in Cherokee] who in a fit of intoxication thrust a butcher knife into the temple of another, Ah-ne-yvng-le, [in Cherokee]."[120] Another case provided "a melancholy comment on the evils of intemperance and Sabbath breaking."[121] George Chapman and Daniel Wright "(both excessively intemperate drinkers)," ended a session of inebriation with Wright dying from being smitten with a shovel and Chapman "awaken[ing] to a sense of the horrid deed he had perpetrated and to the inevitable doom which awaits him."[122] Sway Back was hung following conviction for killing one Murphy with "a large oak stick" while in "a state of extreme intoxication."[123]

As it is in the dominant culture, alcohol abuse remains a serious topic today in Indian Country.[124] In the lands of the Eastern Band of Cherokee Indians, the sale of alcohol is still largely prohibited, except at the casino and certain restaurants, although the lure of the money it can fetch provides political pressure for its allowance.[125]

The Cherokee Supreme Court addressed two alcohol cases. In the first, Samuel Henry was convicted by the jury of selling spiritous liquor and fined one hundred dollars.[126] In the second, Elijah Hicks, a major figure in Cherokee history and, at one point clerk of court, was found guilty of purchasing spirits from a U.S. citizen and given the same fine, which was mandatory, along with $6.00 in costs.[127] The fine was extracted from Mr. Hicks the following year.[128]

Alcohol typically made its way into the Cherokee Nation via the machinations of citizens of the U.S. Peddling liquor was only one of many problems posed by United States citizens within the Cherokee Nation. For example, George Harlan was fined $10.00 by the Supreme Court for hiring an American citizen.[129]

The Cherokee executive and legislative branches used the criminal justice system to enforce a code of morality, including operation to suppress "the great variety of vices emanating from dissipation, particularly from intoxication and gaming at cards."[130] In addition to its cases regulating alcohol, on October 30, 1829, the Cherokee Supreme Court was called upon to fine Thomas J. Pack for "gaming at cards."[131]

One case exemplifies the Cherokee's declining criminal jurisdiction in favor of delivering a suspect to the custody of the United States agent where the United States had an over-arching interest—the alleged crime of counterfeiting U.S. bank notes.[132] The Cherokees used United States currency as their own.[133] Swindlers, cheats, and forgers found their way into the Cherokee Nation with counterfeit currency.[134]

> Some of our neighbors have such a contemptible opinion of us, that they must need not only abuse, but attempt to cheat us, by circulating among us counterfeit money. Their failure in this piece of villainy, however, proves their own ignorance. We have just seen one of these men in the custody of a gentleman from Hightower—he has been arrested for

> having counterfeit bills. He no doubt, times being very hard in Walton County, Georgia, came to make a fortune upon the ignorance of the Indians, for a large bundle (quite an unaccountable thing these times) of these bills was found in his possession. But the Cherokees are not such fools as that comes to—this man was found out in his first attempt at speculation, and is now taken to the agent to receive his reward.[135]

Whether deferring a prosecution from the tribal justice system for prosecution in the courts of the United States was an exception or the rule is difficult to know.

Cherokee Nation v. Georgia demonstrates that the Cherokees were well aware of, and sophisticated litigants within, the courts of the United States.[136] Likewise, it is indisputable that the Secretary of War, and thus the government of the United States, was well aware of the existence of the Cherokee court system.[137]

Not only was the government aware of the Cherokee Supreme Court, its agent sought the assistance of the Court and the sub-agent appeared before it in the investigation of a criminal case in which a citizen of the United States claimed he was robbed by several Cherokees.[138] On April 11, 1829, Thomas Ligon was traveling on the road from Alabama towards Georgia in a two-horse carriage along with a young enslaved person.[139] The road passed through the Cherokee Nation, and in this place was a turnpike or toll road.[140] A heated dispute arose between Mr. Ligon and a number of Cherokees, including one Captain White, regarding payment of the pikeage, or toll.[141] When the dispute ended, Mr. Ligon rode off in his wagon and sought refuge nearby at the residence of one Jacob West, a white man, where he reported that the Cherokees had stolen $1,500.00 from him, a large sum for the times.[142]

After taking Captain White's statement, Agent Montgomery sent a memo to Judge John Martin, still a circuit judge, asking that he "please lend his aid & influence" in obtaining the return of the stolen money.[143] The matter came before Judge Walter Adair, another circuit judge for the Hightower District of the Cherokee Nation.[144] On May 14, 1829, Judge Adair wrote a note that Captain White had appeared and denied the crime, but since no agent "or other person for him" could attend, he deferred the investigation.[145] The case came back for investigation on September 17, 1829, at which time Mr. William Thompson was present as "Agent for Co. Hugh Montgomery."[146] Judge Adair then received testimony from Ah Da Ka Ha Gee, Captain White, and Black Fox.[147] Each witness was then questioned under oath in court by Mr. Thompson.[148]

This striking case and the set of documents which memorialize it, demonstrate that the federal government was willing to use the resources of the tribal courts, including the services of two judges of the Cherokee Supreme Court, to further the interests of the United States. It demonstrates as well that the interests of the United States and that of the Cherokee judicial branch coincided. Nothing about the set of documents demonstrates that this "actual state of things,"[149] agents of the federal government seeking out and appearing before Cherokee Circuit Court judges in a criminal investigation where a citizen of the United States was the alleged victim, was extraordinary. Rather, documents in this case seem to be consistent stylistically with other sworn statements preserved in the Judgment Docket.[150]

On the frontier, access to the courts of the United States might involve a journey of days or even weeks.[151] That agents of the United States government would seek out respectable Cherokee judges for assistance in an urgent situation reflects the pragmatism of the frontier. But it reflects something else, too. This reaching out also underscores that, to the Indian agent, the Cherokee court system was recognized as honorable and trustworthy; its judges were, in fact, judges. It also appears that its jurisdiction was satisfactory to the United States. If it were not, the agents would doubtless have turned elsewhere.

These actions on the part of the Indian agent of the United States were not unique. As early as June of 1824, Agent McMinn advised the Secretary of War that he had turned a white man over to the Cherokee Light Horse[152] for criminal punishment.[153] McMinn did not possess sufficient evidence to bind the defendant, Daniel Rash, over for trial in Knoxville on charges of accessory to robbery because two witnesses would not leave the Cherokee Nation and be subjected to court order to attend in Knoxville.[154]

Stymied, McMinn

> replied that Rash was a proper subject of their laws, and had a right to receive the same penalties that would be inflicted on one of their own proper for a similar offence, the Marshal then observed that by the laws of the Cherokee Nation he would at least be whipped, and asked if I would make any objections [sic] [Upon being told that the agent] would not, the light horse then agreed, and gave him so well as I recollect about 39 lashes laid on with a very tender hand as, I understood.[155]

The significance of this incident should not be underestimated. The agent of the Secretary of War of the United States of America specifically transferred custody of a citizen of the United States to the Cherokee Nation for punishment for a crime committed within the jurisdiction of the Cherokees.[156] The Supreme Court of the United States has yet to analyze tribal court criminal jurisdiction in conjunction with this evidence from the historical record.[157]

Taking these documented recognitions of the sovereignty of the Cherokee people into account necessarily weakens the underpinnings of the *Oliphant* case. These actions by the government suggest something altogether different: that the Cherokees possessed complete criminal jurisdiction.

1. RENNARD STRICKLAND, FIRE AND THE SPIRITS 83, 146 (1975).

2. LAWS OF THE CHEROKEE NATION 99 (spec. ed., Legal Classics Library 1995).

3. JOHN L. DICKSON, THE JUDICIAL HISTORY OF THE CHEROKEE NATION FROM 1721 TO 1835 309 (1964).

4. CHARLOTTE H. PELTIER, THE EVOLUTION OF THE CRIMINAL JUSTICE SYSTEM OF THE EASTERN CHEROKEES 1580–1838 158–159 (1982); DICKSON, *supra* note 3, at 317–18.

5. DICKSON, *supra* note 3, at 333. However, the Constitution did not provide for a Grand Jury to return the bill of indictment. The mechanics of the indictment process remain unclear.

6. *Id.*

7. *Id.*

8. *Id.*

9. *Id.* at 127.

10. *Id.*

11. *See, e.g.*, LAWS OF THE CHEROKEE NATION, *supra* note 2, at 104.

12. A Record Book of the Proceedings of the Supreme Court of the Cherokee Nation (unpublished document, on file with University of Tennessee Institute of Museum and Library Services) [hereinafter Judgment Docket].

13. *Id.*

14. *Id.* at October 16, 1823.

15. *Id.*

16. *Id.*

17. *Id.* at October 29, 1827.

18. *Id.*

19. *Id.*

20. N.C. CONST. art. I, §22; GA. CONST. art. I, §11(c); S.C. CONST. art. I, §11; TENN. CONST. art. I, §14.

21. HENRY T. MALONE, CHEROKEES OF THE OLD SOUTH 83 (1956).

22. *See* Judgment Docket, *supra* note 12.

23. Judgment Docket, *supra* note 12, at November 1, 1824.

24. *Id.*

25. *Id.*

26. Judgment Docket, *supra* note 12, at October 26, 1825.

27. Judgment Docket, *supra* note 12, at October 21, 1825.

28. *See Id.*

29. Judgment Docket, *supra* note 12, at October 28, 1826.

30. *Id.*

31. *Id.*

32. CHEROKEE PHOENIX (New Echota), January 14, 1829.

33. 5 C.J.S. *Appeal and Error* §886 (2009).

34. Judgment Docket, *supra* note 12, at October 24, 1825.

35. *Id.* at October 25, 1825.

36. *Id.* at October 26, 1825.

37. CHEROKEE PHOENIX AND INDIANS' ADVOCATE (New Echota), Jan. 7, 1829.

38. New Echota Historic Site: About North Georgia (October 22, 2009), http://ngeorgia.com/ang/New_Echota_Historic_Site.

39. Malone and Dickson assert that "a jury was required to bring in the court's verdict." MALONE, *supra* note 21, at 83; DICKSON, *supra* note 3, at 315 (citing CHEROKEE PHOENIX, April 10, 1828). However, there is no support for this proposition. And, in any event, review of the Judgment Docket discloses that jury trials were not afforded in every case before the Supreme Court.

40. Judgment Docket, *supra* note 12.

41. *Id.* at October 16, 1827.

42. *Id.* at October 20, 1827.

43. *Id.*

44. LAWS OF THE CHEROKEE NATION, *supra* note 2, at 111.

45. Judgment Docket, *supra* note 12, at November 13, 1828.

46. *Id.* at Oct. 23, 1827

47. *See Id.* at October 21, 1825.

48. *Id.*; *See* Judgment Docket, *supra* note 12, at October 23, 1827.

49. PELTIER, *supra* note 4, at 137.

50. Thomas Lee Ballenger, The Development of Law and Legal Institutions Among the Cherokees 44 (1938) (unpublished Ph.D. dissertation., University of Oklahoma).

51. William Lesley, *Ten Dollars Reward*, CHEROKEE PHOENIX (New Echota), Oct. 29, 1828 (explaining that William Lesley offered a $10.00 reward for the residence of one William Stone, who sold Lesley a mount which later proved to be stolen).

52. SOUTHERN ADVOCATE, CHEROKEE PHOENIX (New Echota), Sept. 24, 1828 (citing from Southern Advocate).

53. Isaac H. Harris, *A Little Too Friendly*, CHEROKEE PHOENIX (New Echota), Nov. 5, 1828.

54. CHEROKEE PHOENIX AND INDIANS' ADVOCATE (New Echota), Feb. 11, 1829.

55. *Id.*

56. *Id.*

57. *Id.*

58. THEDA PERDUE & MICHAEL D. GREEN, THE CHEROKEE NATION AND THE TRAIL OF TEARS 73–74 (2007).

59. Letters Received by the Office of Indian Affairs 1824–1881 Cherokee Agency, East, *microformed on* M-234, reel 72, at 642–55.

60. *Id.*

61. *Id.* at 643–44.

62. *Id.* at 645.

63. *Id.* at 649.

64. *Id.* at 652.

65. Records of the Cherokee Indian Agency in Tennessee, 1801–1835, *microformed on* M-208, reel 10.

66. "Under the new state laws, Cherokees were frequently arrested and detained in the Hall County Jail." TIM A. GARRISON, THE LEGAL IDEOLOGY OF REMOVAL 111 (2002); *see also* State v. Foreman, 16 Tenn. 256 (1835) (holding that the murder of a native Cherokee by a native Cherokee on Cherokee land was subject to the jurisdiction of Tennessee courts); *but see* State v. Ross, 15 Tenn. 74 (1834) (holding that Tennessee did not have the right to tax or regulate residents of the Cherokee Nation); Cornet v. Winston's Lessee, 10 Tenn. 143,

146 (1826) (holding that Cherokees "[a]re in truth a nation of people under the tutelage of the Government of the United States."); Blair v. Pathkiller's Lessee, 10 Tenn. 407 (1830) (holding that a fee estate taken by Tennessee from the United States remained subject to the rights of an individual Cherokee and was thus encumbered).

67. Garrison, *supra* note 66, at 111–24.

68. *Id.*

69. Letters Received by the Office of Indian Affairs 1824–1881 Cherokee Agency, East, *microformed on* M-234, reel 71, at 452–60, 457 (identifying letter of James Williams to the Secretary of War John Calhoun, October 14, 1824).

70. *Id.*

71. *Id.*; Letters Received by the Office of Indian Affairs 1824–1881 Cherokee Agency, East, *microformed on* M-234, reel 71, at 683–86 (identifying letter of Col. Archibald Turk to the Secretary of War John Calhoun, January 6, 1825).

72. George Saunders, Letter to the Editor, Cherokee Phoenix and Indians' Advocate, Dec. 10, 1829, at 2.

73. *Id.*

74. *Id.*

75. *Id.*

76. *Id.*

77. *Id.*

78. *Id.*

79. *Id.*; *see also* Garrison, *supra* note 66, at 111–12 (explaining Judge Clayton's adversarial relationship with the Cherokees).

80. Saunders, *supra* note 72, at 2.

81. *Id.*

82. *Id.*

83. John Ross, *Annual Message*, Cherokee Phoenix and Indians' Advocate, October 16, 1830; *see also* Garrison, *supra* note 66, at 266–267 (discussing John Sanders). Garrison lists Saunders as "John Sanders," perhaps getting the misspelling from Ross's Annual Message or confusing George Saunders for Judge John Sanders, the elected district judge of the Coosawattee District in 1828. It must be the same person, unless the scenario repeated itself. Further, Garrison indicates that Sanders/Saunders was jailed by Judge Clayton, however, Saunders' own account to the *Phoenix* notes that he posted bond at the side of the road.

84. Monroe E. Price, Law and the American Indian 39 (1973).

85. *See Id.*

86. The protection of the courts and the struggle for jurisdiction was not limited to the Cherokee Nation and the neighboring states. Before asserting criminal jurisdiction over non-Indians, the Cherokees "pressed very hard to institute a suit in the Federal Court against a white man charged with having robbed, or stolen two slaves from a native." Records of the Cherokee Indian Agency in Tennessee, 1801–1835, *microformed on* M-208, reel 9 (Letter from Indian Agent McMinn to the Secretary of War, June 24, 1823). Agent McMinn refused this request and instructed the Cherokees to gather their evidence whilst he awaited instructions from the Secretary. *Id.* When the Indians protested that the previous agent, Col. Return J. Meigs, would never have waited for instructions in such circumstances, McMinn reminded the Cherokees that "they were in quite solvent circumstances, and able to support the suit,

which they admitted." *Id.* The Cherokees continued that if the government was willing to pay the expenses of suit, why should their agent oppose the request? *Id.* Agent McMinn advised them that the "Government had determined to curtail its expenses, that it became my duty to aid in lessening expenses." *Id.* In particular, McMinn stated:

> That during their minority, they had a just claim upon the resources of the Govt of the U.States, but that this claim would diminish in the precise ratio, that their Nation, would approximate toward a State of Civilized life, and as a proof, that they were advancing with great rapidity, I referred them to the organization of their nation by which they created laws, and held Courts, and appointed civil officers to carry those laws into execution.

Id. McMinn had already investigated one state court trial involving the murder of a Native that year and delegated a subordinate to sit through another. Records of the Cherokee Indian Agency in Tennessee, 1801–1835, *microformed on* M-208, reel 9 (Letter from Indian Agent McMinn to the Secretary of War, March 6, 1823); Records of the Cherokee Indian Agency in Tennessee, 1801–1835, *microformed on* M-208, reel 9 (Letter from Indian Agent McMinn to Joseph Rogers, May 4, 1823). Thus, in order to avoid the floodgates of litigation and, typically, to save money, the United States, through its own agent, told the Cherokees to use their own courts. Records of the Cherokee Indian Agency in Tennessee, 1801–1835, *microformed on* M-208, reel 9 (Letter from Indian Agent McMinn to the Secretary of War, June 24, 1823). No surprise, then, that they did.

87. Judgment Docket, *supra* note 12, at October 21, 1826.

88. *Id.*

89. Cherokee Phoenix (New Echota), May 21, 1828.

90. Judgment Docket, *supra* note 12, at October 28, 1828.

91. Thievery was also a focus of the *Cherokee Phoenix. See generally,* Cherokee Phoenix (New Echota), July 9, 1828 (noting the occurrences of breaking and entering, larceny and possession of a stolen horse); and George Harlin, *Pocket Book Lost,* Cherokee Phoenix (New Echota), Aug. 13, 1828 (noting an occurrence of pickpocketing).

92. Judgment Docket, *supra* note 12, at October 24, 1828.

93. *Id.*

94. *Id.*

95. *Id.* at October 23, 1827.

96. *Id.* at October 30, 1834.

97. *Id.*

98. Cherokee Phoenix and Indians' Advocate (New Echota), Mar. 18, 1829.

99. Laws of the Cherokee Nation, *supra* note 2, at 104.

100. Judgment Docket, *supra* note 12, at October 21, 1825; October 21, 1829; October 29, 1834.

101. *Id.*

102. Judgment Docket, *supra* note 12, at October, 21, 1825.

103. *Id.* at October 29, 1834; *See generally* Laws of the Cherokee Nation, *supra* note 2, at 103 (stating that murder cases required twelve jurors).

104. Judgment Docket, *supra* note 12, at October 21, 1829.

105. *Id.*; Cherokee Phoenix and Indians' Advocate (New Echota), Feb. 24, 1830 (stating that the National Council provided that "a respite of five days shall be allowed to the criminal after sentence of death shall be passed, before he shall be executed").

106. *See* Judgment Docket, *supra* note 12.

107. *Id.*; Cherokee Phoenix and Indians' Advocate (New Echota), Oct. 21, 1829.

108. Cherokee Phoenix and Indians' Advocate (New Echota), Oct. 21, 1829.

109. *Id.*

110. *Id.*

111. *Id.*

112. *Id.*

113. Laws of the Cherokee Nation, *supra* note 2, at 133.

114. Cherokee Phoenix and Indians' Advocate (New Echota), Oct. 21, 1829.

115. Theda Perdue, *Clan and Court: Another Look at the Early Cherokee Republic*, 24 Am. Indian Q. 562, 567 (2000).

116. *See also* the case of James Pettit, discussed *supra* at pp. 44–46, 48, for another example of the exercise of criminal jurisdiction over a non-Indian, this time by the National Committee.

117. Cherokee Phoenix and Indians' Advocate (New Echota), Oct. 21, 1829.

118. Intervention of the National Council on behalf of a criminal defendant was not unprecedented, despite a law enacted on October 17, 1823, which attempted to channel litigation into the courts and away from the Council and National Committee. Laws of the Cherokee Nation, *supra* note 2, at 31–32. On October 27, 1825, the Committee agreed with the Council and enacted a special law on behalf of Samuel Henry, remitting his Court imposed fine for introducing brandy into the Nation. *Id.* at 49.

119. Theda Perdue, Cherokee Women: Gender and Culture Change, 1700 to 1835 151 (1998).

120. Unknown Author, *Unknown Title*, Cherokee Phoenix (New Echota), Sept. 17, 1828.

121. Cherokee Phoenix (New Echota), Aug. 27, 1828.

122. *Id.*

123. Cherokee Phoenix (New Echota), Apr. 24, 1828.

124. Scott McKie B.P., *Alcohol Vote Could Occur as Early as June*, The Cherokee One Feather (Cherokee), Dec. 24, 2008 at A1, A5.

125. *Id.*

126. Judgment Docket, *supra* note 12, at October 21, 1825.

127. *Id.* at November 3, 1826; Laws of the Cherokee Nation, *supra* note 2, at 104.

128. Judgment Docket, *supra* note 12, at October 18, 1927.

129. Judgment Docket, *supra* note 12, at October 22, 1829.

130. Laws of the Cherokee Nation, *supra* note 2, at 26.

131. Judgment Docket, *supra* note 12, at October 30, 1829; Laws of the Cherokee Nation, *supra* note 2, at 96 (noting that gaming at dice, roulette, or thimbles was also prohibited).

132. Cherokee Phoenix and Indians' Advocate (New Echota), Feb. 24, 1830.

133. *Id.*

134. *Id.*

135. *Id.*

136. Cherokee Nation v. Georgia, 30 U.S. 1 (1831).

137. On January 6, 1830, Agent Hugh Montgomery advised the secretary of a claim by one Henry Gill against the Cherokee Nation for the theft of money by some unknown

Cherokee. Included in the materials submitted were two depositions made by white men before "one of the Indian Judges." Letters received by the Office of Indian Affairs, Cherokee Agency East, 1824–1881, *microformed on* M-234, reel 74, at 212–13 (identifying letter from Indian Agent Montgomery to the Secretary of War, January 6, 1830).

138. Letters received by the Office of Indian Affairs, Cherokee Agency East, 1824–1881, *microformed on* M-234, reel 73, at 767–85 (identifying multiple court documents, including the following: Cherokee Circuit Court records from the Hightower District, September 17, 1829; Statement of Thomas Ligon to Agent Hugh Montgomery, April 16, 1829; Memorandum of Agent Hugh Montgomery to Judge John Martin, April 16, 1829; Memorandum of Judge Walter Adair, May 14, 1829; letter from ___ Vann to Judge Walter Adair, September 16, 1829).

139. Letters received by the Office of Indian Affairs, Cherokee Agency East, 1824–1881, *microformed on* M-234, reel 73, at 767–71 (letter identifying statement of Thomas Ligon to Agent Hugh Montgomery, April 16, 1829).

140. *Id.*

141. Letters, *supra* note 138.

142. Letters received by the Office of Indian Affairs, Cherokee Agency East, 1824–1881, *microformed on* M-234, reel 73, at 767–71 (letter identifying statement of Thomas Ligon to Agent Hugh Montgomery, April 16, 1829).

143. Letters received by the Office of Indian Affairs, Cherokee Agency East, 1824–1881, *microformed on* M-234, reel 73, at 771 (citing from the Memorandum of Agent Hugh Montgomery to Judge John Martin, April 16, 1829).

144. Letters received by the Office of Indian Affairs, Cherokee Agency East, 1824–1881, *microformed on* M-234, reel 73 (citing from the Memorandum of Judge Walter Adair, May 14, 1829).

145. *Id.*

146. Letters received by the Office of Indian Affairs, Cherokee Agency East, 1824–1881, *microformed on* M-234, reel 73, at 774–85, 779 (citing from the Cherokee Circuit Court records from the Hightower District, September 17, 1829).

147. *Id.* at 774–85.

148. *Id.*

149. Johnson v. M'Intosh, 21 U.S. 543, 589 (1823).

150. Judgment Docket, *supra* note 12, at October 30, 1829.

151. *Id.*

152. The Cherokee Light Horse had existed since the turn of the nineteenth century as a kind of mobile police/paramilitary force. By the time of Agent McMinn's letter to the Secretary of War the law provided for "one company of light-horse to accompany each circuit judge on his official duties, in his respective districts, and to execute such punishment on thieves as the judges and Council shall decide, agreeably to law...." Cherokee Phoenix (New Echota), March 27, 1828; Theda Perdue & Michael D. Green, The Cherokee Nation and the Trail of Tears 36 (2007).

153. Letters received by the Office of Indian Affairs, Cherokee Agency East, 1824–1881, *microformed on* M-234, reel 71, at 260–66 (identifying the letter from Indian Agent McMinn to the Secretary of War John Calhoun, June 9, 1824).

154. *Id.*

155. Letters received by the Office of Indian Affairs, Cherokee Agency East, 1824–1881, *microformed on* M-234, reel 71, at 260–66, 263 (identifying the letter from Indian Agent McMinn to the Secretary of War John Calhoun, June 9, 1824); One of the Marshal's duties was "to execute the decisions of the judges in their respective districts." *See generally* CHEROKEE PHOENIX (New Echota), March 27, 1828.

156. Letters received by the Office of Indian Affairs, Cherokee Agency East, 1824–1881, *microformed on* M-234, reel 71, at 260–66 (identifying the letter from Indian Agent McMinn to the Secretary of War John Calhoun, June 9, 1824).

157. *See* Plains Commerce Bank v. Long Family Land & Cattle Co., 554 U.S. 316 (2008); Nevada v. Hicks, 533 U.S. 353 (2001); Strate v. A-1 Contractors, 520 U.S. 438 (1997); Montana v. United States, 450 U.S. 544 (1981); United States v. Lara, 541 U.S. 193 (2004); Cherokee Nation v. Georgia, 30 U.S. 1 (1831); United States v. Wheeler, 435 U.S. 313 (1978); Duro v. Reina, 496 U.S. 676 (1998); Oliphant v. Suquamish Indian Tribe, 435 U.S. 191 (1978); Talton v. Mayes, 163 U.S. 376 (1896); Ex Parte Crow Dog, 109 U.S. 556 (1883); Johnson v. M'Intosh, 21 U.S. (8 Wheat.) 543 (1823).

Interior scene of the Samuel Worcester house, which still stands at the New Echota Historic Site, Calhoun, GA.

7

The Civil Jurisprudence of the Court

The civil docket comprised the majority of the Supreme Court's work. Excluding slavery, these cases are readily identifiable to the modern practitioner: damages for contracts and torts, debt collection, ejectment, allegations of swindling, trespassing, rights in personal property, damages to real property, assault and battery, and an action on a bond. The cases ranged from the mundane (a debt of $8.00) to the exotic (a lawsuit over possession of peacock feathers). The claims present such ancient common law actions as trover and replevin in contrast with seemingly modern concepts as arbitration. As might be expected in such a rural jurisdiction, actions over the right to horses held a prominence. Similarly, claims for livestock and crops occupied significant time of the Court.

As the National Committee became more and more involved in the affairs of state and in the increasingly desperate actions to forestall removal, more and more disputes—matters which would have earlier been resolved locally, either at the clan or town level—were assigned to the court system, both formally by way of statutes and informally by referral. Thus, as the organization of the nation grew more centralized, the power and scope of the Court broadened accordingly.

The Supreme Court was busy almost immediately. Even though there were no formalized processes for executing or collecting on a judgment until November 12, 1825, when the National Committee enacted a law setting out a framework for execution,[1] users eagerly adopted the new system. For example, on October 15, 1823, the Supreme Court found Joseph Crutchfield liable to Robert Vann in the sum of twenty dollars. Almost a decade later, on October 2, 1833, this judgment was marked "Satisfied." While we often boil down rule of law into the catch phrase "fair and impartial courts," civil society must also have mechanisms with which to manifest the considered judgments of the fair and impartial courts. In this way, the obligations of the rights of contracting parties are made enforceable and those damaged by the torts of others have meaningful redress. The sale of property to satisfy judgments was one way: "The court often ordered slaves sold in satisfaction of debts and judgments and in settlement of estates. The *Phoenix* carried announcements of approaching sales."[2] Another satisfactory way was for the Court simply to award ownership in a contested item. For an example of both, on Monday, October 18, 1830, the Widow Cornblade sued James Fields to recover possession of a horse. "The Court [found] for the plaintiff the horse contended for or fifty dollars in trade at valuation."[3]

In addition to the Supreme Court's adjudicatory framework, it also served as the repository for the recordation and discharge of its own judgments. With such a structure, commercial activity could be engaged in with confidence. Although a decade would pass before Joseph Crutchfield's judgment debt to Robert Vann was paid, the fact that the judgment was ultimately satisfied demonstrates that the Court was open and that the parties, plaintiff and defendant, accepted its authority and ultimately acceded to it.

One reason for that acceptance is structural: Supreme Court had the full complement of inherent authority. On November 8, 1828, the National Committee and Council enacted a law formalizing this authority:

> That the Judges of the several Courts in the Nation shall have the power to adopt such rules and regulations, as shall be necessary to preserve good order in their Courts, and to punish those who shall be guilty of disorderly behavior in contempt of the Court, by imposing such fines as in their opinion shall be deemed justifiable, *provided*, that the same shall not exceed ten dollars for each offense.[4]

The Supreme Court used it, at least once, fining John Broward one dollar for the offence of contempt of court.[5]

In his seminal work on the subject, Dean Felix Stumpf argued:

> [t]he lack of any separation of powers, which would insulate tribal judges from retaliation by their councils, has been viewed as a major shortcoming of tribal courts and therefore militates against any recognition of the existence of inherent powers in these courts.[6]

However, Article 2, Section 2 of the Cherokee Constitution of 1827 specifically established the separation of powers between the legislative, executive, and judicial branches of the Nation's government: "No person or persons belonging to one of these shall exercise any of the powers properly belonging to either of the others, except in the cases hereinafter expressly directed or permitted."[7] This being the case, Dean Stumpf would argue that, having "achieved freedom from [its] councils" the Cherokee Supreme Court "should [have been] able to exercise inherent powers" at the time of the ratification of the Constitution.[8] The legislation of 1828 simply formalized it.

The Court's usage of its inherent authority in its civil jurisdiction is wonderfully illustrated in the case of *Richard Fields and Nathan Hicks v. John Ross.*[9] On June 15, 1825, the National Committee and Council enacted legislation establishing that "[t]he several courts of justice in the Nation shall have no cognizance of any case transpiring previous to the organization of courts by law."[10] Nonetheless, in the 1827 case of *Fields and Hicks v. Ross*, the Supreme Court held: "The Court decide that the Courts of Justice have cognisance [sic] of cases transpiring as far back as the year one thousand and eight hundred 1800—."[11] Although it does not trumpet it, this decision is the Cherokee Supreme Court's version of *Marbury v. Madison.*[12] In effect, through the use of its inherent powers, in this decision the Cherokee Supreme Court voided an act of the legislative branch of government and established its own time frame for exercise of jurisdiction. This is the mark of a court fully in control of its powers, defining its own authority.

While the devolution of the judicial power to the Supreme Court occurred incrementally as the nation grew increasingly sophisticated, legally, the Court grew in stature and in acceptance as the agreed arbiter of civil disputes. In the inverse of white Americans subjected to the criminal process of the tribal courts, the evidence suggests that white Americans actively sought redress in the Cherokee Supreme Court for civil matters.

James Turk was an early settler of Maryville, Tennessee, where he became known as a saddler and a tanner, and where he owned a stable.[13] He occupied multiple positions in society and the government there, including director of the Maryville Bank, and, in 1822, justice of the peace.[14] He subsequently moved to McMinn County, Tennessee, where he helped establish the early county government.[15] He owned a trading post in the Cherokee Nation[16] and from that vantage point must have been familiar with the Cherokee Supreme Court. Sometime prior to October 1828, Turk obtained a judgment in McMinn County, Tennessee, against C and JW Agnew. The Agnews are unknown, although it is likely that they were white Americans. A John Agnew was one of the "fortunate drawers" in the lottery of Cherokee Georgian lands prior to the removal.[17] However, Cherokees bought and sold land in Tennessee during this time period as free persons of color,[18] and so the Agnews may have been Cherokee. In any event, Turk concluded that the Agnews held property within the Cherokee Nation upon which he could levy execution of his Tennessee judgment. So, he sought to docket his McMinn County judgment in the Cherokee Supreme Court and to sue to collect on it as a valid debt. The case came on for hearing on Thursday, November 13, 1828, and the Cherokee Supreme Court held for the defendants.[19] This marks the earliest known attempt to enforce a state court judgment in Indian Country. It is also the first known instance of a non-Indian directly seeking a civil judgment in a tribal court.

It was not the last. In one of the largest lawsuits entertained by the Cherokee Supreme Court, the Alabama corporation Wyckoff, Pickens & Co. sued Andrew Ross, the brother of Principal Chief John Ross, and Elizabeth Pack on the alleged default of a debt on a promissory note.[20] Wyckoff, Pickens & Co. was a corporation of cotton traders who, in the late 1820s, regularly shipped cotton by steamboat from Selma to Mobile on the Alabama River and received merchandise in return.[21] Surviving accounts demonstrate the corporation to have been comprised of confident traders, not adverse to risk, and well represented by able counsel.[22] It is possible that the corporation was represented by the attorney E. Pickens, who appeared for the company in two reported cases in the Alabama Supreme Court.[23] When the case came on for trial before the Cherokee Supreme Court, the judges entered judgment in favor of the corporation against Andrew Ross and Elizabeth Pack in the sum of $2,173.69 plus the costs of the lawsuit, an enormous sum for the day.[24] In November 1829, the marshal received the issued execution.[25] That a substantial Selma, Alabama, corporation could come into the tribal court and obtain such a judgment is an enduring testament to the validity of the Cherokee Supreme Court. This is the first known appearance of an American corporation in a tribal court.

These cases vividly illustrate that the Cherokee Supreme Court was accepted not just internally, by the Cherokee people, but also externally, by white Americans, as the frontier receded, and a new, mercantile class arose around the Cherokee nation. By regulating interstate commerce in this fashion, the Supreme Court operated as the court system of a completely sovereign state. The prospect of an Indian court adjudicating the affairs of white Americans terrified and revolted the Georgians in particular.[26] The Georgians feared the recognition of an alien government existing on land they believed was rightfully theirs.

> In order to reaffirm state power over territory within the Cherokee nation, the Georgia legislature abolished the Cherokee government and prohibited the council from meeting. The state legislature extended Georgia law to include the Cherokees, passed a series of discriminatory acts that forbade the Cherokees from mining their own gold, from using their own court system, and from testifying against

whites in Georgia courts. The state then created a special police force, the Georgia Guard, to enforce these laws among the Cherokees.[27]

The role of the Cherokee Supreme Court in provoking the Georgian backlash has not been fully extrapolated. When a white American like Turk would seek to docket a foreign judgment in the tribal court, he was treating the Cherokee nation as a state and willingly submitting to the powers and processes of its jurisdiction. When a foreign corporation filed an original action in the tribal court, seeking damages from tribal members, it did likewise. These examples, one from Tennessee and one from Alabama, demonstrate an acceptance and a growing evolution of the Cherokee Supreme Court into a mature, respected court, one trusted with significant concerns in interstate commerce between the people of the United States and the Indian nation.

The Georgians could not tolerate this for their citizens. What if the Cherokees attempted to adjudicate Georgian property rights in their courts? The result for Georgia would be unthinkable. Although many paths led to the Trail of Tears, the Cherokee Supreme Court unwittingly, and by its own stunning success, helped put the tribe on the road to removal.

The Supreme Court of the United States has never considered the fact that American mercantile interests willingly submitted to the jurisdiction of the Cherokee Supreme Court in the 1820s. Such an historical fact upends much of the Supreme Court's jurisprudence in this area—that white Americans historically never made use of the tribal courts and certainly should be hailed into them only in certain highly constrained circumstances. These examples suggest that a reevaluation of some of the doctrinal structures of federal Indian law is overdue.

While the revelation that the Supreme Court spanned cultural, racial, and territorial boundaries in its short tenure is paradigm shifting, an equal significance of its civil jurisprudence may be its role in the maintenance of a framework regarding real property.

To this day, a myth persists that the Cherokees did not own land, but rather used it collectively. This myth is an offshoot of the notion of the "noble savage," aboriginal people frolicking in an idyllic, sylvan world of hunting and gathering, where game and other fruits of the land abounded. Indeed, this is the very vision adopted the by the Supreme Court of the United States in the seminal case of *Johnson v. M'Intosh.*[28] In this case the Court held that, as Indians did not use lands as the Europeans did, they were subject to being defeased through the "Doctrine of Discovery," where their "discovery" of and subsequent "conquest" by Europeans nullified any title (as the Europeans understood it) to land in the United States they might have held. This, the reasoning went, left them with only a right to possess lands, which they could not sell to anyone but the federal government, since it, after all, really owned the Indian lands.[29]

For the Cherokees, land ownership was much more nuanced.

> Indigenous Cherokee law distinguished between two kinds of real property—hunting grounds and fields. Cherokees owned the hunting grounds communally, and each man was equally bound to defend this property from any encroachment. Not even a chief could sell this land because "no Indian, however great his influence and authority, could give away more than his own right to any tract of land, which, in proportion, is no more than as one man to the whole tribe." On the other hand, Cherokees originally considered an individual's house and fields to belong to him personally, or to his lineage, and the owner could dispose of his holdings at will.[30]

This nuance goes far beyond what a European would consider as a fee ownership, reaching into the realm of the spirit. In drawing some general conclusions, Loftin has stated that "Native American tribes do not perceive the spiritual as distinct from their land. Their land and religion are one."[31] In this way, the idea of land becomes very different between native and Anglo cultures.

As the pressure for land cessation and then removal grew, however, the Cherokees formally changed their traditional laws, in essence "apply[ing] the rules of communal ownership to" homesteads and reducing what had been a personal belonging to purely a possessory interest.[32] The Cherokees enshrined this as a matter of constitutional law in Article I, Section 2 of the Constitution of 1827:

> The sovereignty and Jurisdiction of this Government shall extend over the country within the boundaries above described, and the lands therein are, and shall remain, the common property of the Nation; but the improvements made thereon, and in the possession of the citizens of the Nation, are the exclusive and indefeasible property of the citizens respectively who made; or may rightfully be in possession of them.[33]

Nonetheless, the Cherokee Supreme Court consistently continued to consider real property cases as if the underlying land were owned individually. For example, on Wednesday, October 28, 1829, the Supreme Court heard Elizabeth Sutton's case against Thomas Berry and Rick Edmonson "to recover for a plantation."[34] The Court held for the defense and ordered "the National Office to take possession of the plantation."[35] A similar suit by John Baldridge against Jesse Raper was "[d]ismissed by default."[36] Jesse Raper was sitting at the plaintiff's table a few days later, where he sued for possession of a plantation and lost.[37] On Wednesday, October 20, 1830, the Court ruled in favor of the plaintiff, Crying Snake, in a suit over a field near Pathkiller's ferry.[38] In the next case, the Court found "for the Plaintiff the field and houses in dispute." A few days later, the Court settled a boundary dispute:

> The Court decide the corner starting from a pine tree on the hill and running a straight line direction to the mouth of the hollow, near the corner of Post's field dividing between the properties shall be the true line, and that the National Marshal as soon as convenient proceed to the place notifying the parties & mark the line.[39]

In this way, the Cherokee Supreme Court worked to normalize real property law within the nation in a way that conformed with Cherokee culture and tradition. While the national government may have decreed that all the land was held communally, the Court acted, particularly in drawing boundaries and entertaining suits for possession of tracts of property, as if the government had not. In this way, traditional notions of real property could be maintained, even if, to the outside world, they had been abandoned. Once again, the Court, a modern, Anglo construct, worked to maintain an undercurrent of traditional life internally.

This is not to suggest that the Supreme Court ignored the property laws. For example, while the Court was initially open to resolving cases involving ferries,[40] following the enactment of the Constitution of 1827, the Court was clear that the national government retained control over turnpikes, roads, and ferries, and therefore such claims were not justiciable in the court system.[41] Similarly, the Court was fastidious in hewing to the statute passed on November 12, 1824,[42] prohibiting improvements within a quarter of a mile from the field or plantation of another, when it directed the sheriff of the district to appoint two disinterested men to inspect the property physically in such a case.[43]

The Cherokee Supreme Court was both an outward- and inward-looking court in the exercise of its civil jurisdiction as in other aspects of its operation. In its exercise of its inherent authority and in its willingness to entertain matters filed by non-tribal members (aliens actually), it was demonstrably modern, particularly for a court that began on what was the fringe of the American frontier. On the other hand, in its protection of individual property rights, the Court perpetuated cultural and traditional norms ostensibly supplanted by legislation.

Both of these courses charted by the Court led to an increased acceptance of it. This acceptance was one of the reasons that the judicial system was almost immediately reconstituted in the Indian Territory following the removal.

1. LAWS OF THE CHEROKEE NATION 59–60 (spec. ed., Legal Classics Library 1995).

2. Theda Perdue, *Cherokee Planters, in* THE CHEROKEE INDIAN NATION: A TROUBLED HISTORY 124, (Duane H. King, Ed. 1979); *see also* LAWS OF THE CHEROKEE NATION, *supra* note 1, 79, 97–98.

3. A Record Book of the Proceedings of the Supreme Court of the Cherokee Nation (unpublished document, on file with University of Tennessee Institute of Museum and Library Services) at Monday, October 18, 1830 [hereinafter Judgment Docket].

4. LAWS OF THE CHEROKEE NATION, *supra* note 1, at 101.

5. Judgment Docket, *supra* note 3, at Monday, October 26, 1835.

6. FELIX F. STUMPF, INHERENT POWERS OF THE COURT 20–21 (2008).

7. LAWS OF THE CHEROKEE NATION, *supra* note 1, at 120; *see also Id.* at 46 (the fixed and "irrevocable principle" of government, foreshadowing the Constitution).

8. STUMPF, *supra* note 6, at 21.

9. Judgment Docket, *supra* note 3, at Friday, October 26, 1827.

10. LAWS OF THE CHEROKEE NATION, *supra* note 1, at 120.

11. Judgment Docket, *supra* note 3, at Friday, October 26, 1827. This jurisdictional "look back" makes sense. Naturally, cases began to accrue prior to the existence of the Cherokee Supreme Court. Cases accruing prior to 1800 could not be entertained by the Court jurisdictionally. This not the same as a statute of limitations, such as the two-year period for demand of payment under a contract enacted on October 17, 1825. The Supreme Court adhered to this in the case of Hetty Vickry v. Darcus Hummingbird: "The Court decide in favor of the defendant as debarred by the limitation act". Judgment Docket, *supra* note 3, at Thursday, October 29, 1829.

12. Marbury v. Madison, 5 U.S. (1 Cranch) 137 (1803).

13. *Blount County from Godspeed's 1887 History of Tennessee*, (March 3, 2014) http://www.tennesseegenealogy.org/blount2/History.html; *see also* Edna Barney, *~Notes~*, TURKS OF VIRGINIA (2002), http://www.ednabarney.com/docs/turknotes.html#31.

14. Edna Barney, *~Notes~*, TURKS OF VIRGINIA (2002), http://www.ednabarney.com/docs/turknotes.html#31.

15. *Id.*

16. *Id.*

17. JAMES F. SMITH, THE CHEROKEE LAND LOTTERY CONTAINING A NUMERICAL LIST OF THE NAMES OF THE FORTUNATE DRAWERS IN SAID LOTTERY WITH AN ENGRAVED MAP OF EACH DISTRICT 353 (1838) (ebook) https://books.google.com/books?id=4fQxAQAAMAAJ&pg=PA353&lpg=PA353&dq=John+Agnew+Cherokee&source=bl&ots=5SkfB8QN70&sig=uNh9y0HHk8NDr9QKXmFUD9AEtiM&hl=en&sa=X&ved=0ahUKEwj_orLMnLrYAhUjxYMKHeCjCsQQ6AEIODAD#v=onepage&q=John%20Agnew%20Cherokee&f=false.

18. MCMINN COUNTY, TENNESSEE DEEDS: DEED BOOK A 5–67 (January 6, 2003), http://www.tngenweb.org/records/mcminn/land/pg5-67.htm.

19. Judgment Docket, *supra* note 3, at Thursday, November 13, 1828.

20. Judgment Docket, *supra* note 3, at Saturday, October 17, 1829.

21. WALTER M. JACKSON, THE STORY OF SELMA 83–85 (1954).

22. *See, e.g.*, Wyckoff, Pickens & Co. v. Taylor, 2 AL 105 (1832); Harrison v. Marshall, 6 AL (6 Porter 65) 417 (1837); https://www.wikitree.com/wiki/Higginbotham-97.

23. *Id.*

24. Judgment Docket, *supra* note 3, at Saturday, October 17, 1829.

25. *Id.*

26. Indeed it happened. On Saturday, October 23, 1830, M. Hildebrand's case against James Pettit was heard in the Supreme Court. Of course, Pettit had been sued earlier in the Court by his wife.

27. Theda Perdue, The Cherokee 55 (1989). These December, 1828 laws led directly to what are now known as The Cherokee Cases, Cherokee Nation v. Georgia, 30 U.S. (5 Pet.) 1 (1831) and Worcester v. Georgia, 31 U.S. (6 Pet.) 515 (1832), cases which crushed the Cherokees' hopes that the Supreme Court of the United States or the executive branch would come to their aid, yet, ultimately proved to be the foundation of modern federal Indian law.

28. Johnson v. M'Intosh, 21 U.S. (8 Wheat.) 543 (1823).

29. This remains the law of the land, and, ironically in the twenty-first century, Indian Tribes deed land to the federal government to hold in trust for them, much as envisioned in *Johnson*, to protect it from encroachment by the states, and, until recently, as a way to establish Tribal lands for Indian gaming. *See* J. Matthew Martin, *The Supreme Court Erects a Fence Around Indian Gaming*, 39 Okla. City L. Rev. 46 (2014).

30. Theda Perdue, *Cherokee Planters: The Development of Plantation Slavery Before Removal*, *in* The Cherokee Indian Nation: A Troubled History 114 (Duane King, ed. 1979) (citation omitted).

31. John D. Loftin, *Anglo-American Jurisprudence and the Native American Tribal Quest for Religious Freedom*, 13 Am. Indian Culture and Res. J. 1, 2 (1989).

32. *Id.* at 114–15.

33. Laws of the Cherokee Nation, *supra* note 1, at 119.

34. Judgment Docket, *supra* note 3, at Wednesday, October 28, 1829.

35. *Id.*

36. *Id.*

37. Judgment Docket, *supra* note 3, at Saturday, October 31, 1829.

38. Judgment Docket, *supra* note 3, at Wednesday, October 20, 1830.

39. Judgment Docket, *supra* note 3, at Saturday, October 23, 1830.

40. Judgment Docket, *supra* note 3, at Friday, October 27, 1826.

41. Judgment Docket, *supra* note 3, at Thursday, October 25, 1827.

42. Laws of the Cherokee Nation, *supra* note 1, at 40.

43. Judgment Docket, *supra* note 3, at Thursday, October 29, 1835.

Samuel Worcester house, as it appears today, New Echota Historic Site, Calhoun, GA.

8

Conclusion

Those who study human behavior have come to realize that the justice system of the United States is infected with implicit bias.[1] "In light of the evidence linking implicit bias to a variety of discriminatory outcomes, legal scholars and empiricists must deeply consider the various ways in which implicit bias may affect all areas of the law in which disparities appear."[2] Among others, these effects may include ingroup preferences and implicit racial biases.[3] Federal Indian law is hardly immune. Professor Pommersheim has noted that Indian tribes are extra constitutional entities.[4] As such, tribal courts are certainly not part of the ingroup. Indeed, tribal courts' very "otherness" is a cause of significant confusion about and limitation of these tribunals' functionality. Racial notions of indigenous people continue to be part of the daily headlines in American legal reportage and framed a significant part of nineteenth century jurisprudence. A prime current example are the ongoing developments regarding the names and likenesses of professional sports teams.

Since 1978, the pillars of the Supreme Court of the United States' jurisprudence on the sovereignty of the various tribes, including the civil and criminal jurisdiction of the tribal courts, has been a quintessentially ingroup notion—that the tribes, and by extension, the tribal courts, are too undeveloped, too alien, and too extra constitutional to do much more than adjudicate some but not all of the affairs of their members. Time and again, the Supreme Court of the United States has struggled to contextualize a framework where the affairs of non-Indian citizens of the United States[5] within Indian Country may be subject to tribal justice. This is a struggle not just for sovereignty, but for the very heart of Indian Country.

From the beginning, the Supreme Court of the United States has been troubled that normal rules simply do not work in construing the relationships between the indigenous population and the ascendant American Constitution.

To conceptualize the problem, outside of an operative rule, the Supreme Court of the United States sought to ascertain "the actual state of things."[6] This continues to this day as the Court experiments with a pastiche of statutes, treaties, and federal common law in order to reach and understand "the current state of affairs."[7]

Understanding "the current state of affairs," or "the actual state of things," cannot be done without a more complete understanding of our shared legal histories. To understand what powers Indian tribes in general and the Cherokees in particular possessed and continue to possess, twenty-first century federal courts must have access to the legal histories of these peoples and their territories. Put simply, the federal courts must know what they did.

"History is, by and large, a record of what people did, not what they failed to do: to this extent it is inevitably a success story."[8] The success story of the Cherokee Supreme Court is a legal history. Heretofore, historians—not legal historians—have—quite properly—commented on the Cherokee Supreme Court as an exemplar of the rapid transformation of Cherokee society in a desperate effort to forestall removal. However, these observations miss the larger and much more significant point: the Cherokee Supreme Court as an exemplar of the first written legal narrative of tribal jurisprudence.[9] The legal narrative is what drove the Court, gave it a reason for being, and propelled it to be reconstituted in the Indian Territory following the Trail of Tears, when there was no need to retain it, if it existed only as a hedge against removal.

Justice Richland investigated legal narrativity, integrated into a model by which he could analyze Hopi courtroom interaction as a reflection "of the shape and contour of Hopi law as an enduring institution in Hopi social life."[10] This reflection, hitched to anthropological narrative models, "illuminate[s] the everyday constitution of Hopi law as an enduring structure of Hopi social action."[11]

Similarly, the record of Cherokee Supreme Court decisions, case dispositions enduring over the centuries, becomes such a model when analyzed by legal historians. Thus, the dual narrative of history becomes the discursive force, illuminating not only the construction of Westernized Cherokee law as a new structure within the social framework of both Cherokee and American society, but also as a bulwark protecting the more ancient, indigenous culture undergirding it. From this perspective, these stories become "public stor[ies],"[12] tales of both the litigants as well as of those who joined together in the joint creation, for the first time, of official, written, judge-made, aboriginal law.

This narrative duality simultaneously shields tribal culture and tradition but also hampers tribal sovereignty as reliability, suggested as consistency by the Congress of the United States,[13] is multiplied by 574 federally recognized tribes, each with its own organic, aboriginal law in the form of custom and tradition and each with its own individualized, formalistic, governmental experience, whether that be statutes, ordinances, or other unique frameworks. The expectations of Congress lead to a Hobson's choice for Indian Nations: either the tribal court is so Westernized that it loses popular support at home because it abandons the old ways altogether, or the processes are so alien that the dominant government in Washington cannot stomach them.[14]

The actions of the original Cherokee Supreme Court demonstrate that this duality existed from the beginning of the tribal courts:

> What historians do is an abstraction of what has happened in the past. In what really happened, setting aside cosmogony, there are no beginnings and no endings. There are no limits to the breadth of phenomena that might have affected what happened. To play off a line in the play *Inherit the Wind*, there really is a creation in the next county that might affect any given story. But historians have to draw the line somewhere in order to try to understand the most important drivers of what happened. From this they stitch together a plausible story that we can understand.[15]

The most plausible story of the Cherokee Supreme Court is not one of a mere vehicle of social change in a doomed effort to forestall removal,[16] but rather of a court with complete jurisdiction, using virtually all the powers we associate with a modern court. At the same time, the Court operated in such a way as to preserve certain tribal traditions—the nature of property, the role of women, the existence of the clan structure—indeed, what it meant to be Cherokee. The Cherokee Supreme Court and the judicial system over which it presided then was far more than a footnote; rather, in a time of existential crisis for the Cherokee people, it became a storehouse of written law, both legislative and judge-made, and also of valuable components of tribal custom and tradition. With all that was lost in the genocide, doubtless far more would have disappeared but for that repository of law and norms.

Although master storytellers, as an outgroup, the Cherokees have lacked both political power and narrative control to advance their tales of justice beyond their own territories. Indeed, all indigenous people have, almost from the very beginning of the United States. "The big problem that arises in American Indian legal studies is transliterating Native American categories into Anglo-American legal discourse."[17] To this day, law students are stunned to realize that, in *Johnson v. M'Intosh*, no Indian was a party to the lawsuit that decreed that Indians could not own property and thus, all natives were defeased.

As a result, ingroup notions papered over the history of tribal justice and erroneous assumptions assumed positions as the basis of law. Even something as elemental as the quest for truth is impacted. "For Native American tribes, truth is mythological; for Anglo jurists it is logical."[18]

Times are changing and new voices are being raised. Another story, one more plausible as the "actual state of things," should be presented to the Supreme Court of the United States. In this story, the Cherokee Supreme Court was a court of competent jurisdiction, which it exercised over white Americans at their request and, like its state counterparts, over African-Americans to their detriment. This Court had a full complement of modern powers, like the contempt power, the power to order cases into arbitration, and, as its lower courts demonstrated, the power to exercise criminal jurisdiction over white Americans, even at the request of the federal government. This view of law should lead to a new story, a new understanding of "the current state of affairs," because if an Indian tribe had such powers in the 1820s and 1830s, powers so vast that the very sovereignty of Georgia was deemed threatened, they are an indelible sign of retained aboriginal sovereignty. This story threatens to undercut the very foundations of federal Indian law for the last forty years. From the old, ingroup story: tribal courts never did such things. To the new but more plausible outgroup story: yes, they did. Then change, or at least a new and different authority, must substitute to explain "the current state of affairs."

When this happens, the stories of the brave women and men who created the Cherokee Supreme Court and made it their own will once again be heard, and their works will continue to resonate with a new significance, two centuries after they began. In this way, "The noble knights of the Bar of the East Side"[19] take their rightful place as actors in a new story of sovereignty.

1. ENHANCING JUSTICE REDUCING BIAS (Sarah E. Redfield ed., 2017).

2. Justin D. Levinson, Danielle M. Young, & Laurie A. Rudman, *Implicit Bias a Social Science Overview*, ENHANCING JUSTICE REDUCING BIAS 58 (Sarah E. Redfield ed., 2017).

3. Andrew J. Wistrich and Jeffrey J. Rachlinski, *Implicit Bias in Judicial Decision Making*, ENHANCING JUSTICE REDUCING BIAS 98–104 (Sarah E. Redfield ed., 2017).

4. FRANK POMMERSHEIM, BROKEN LANDSCAPE 61 (2009).

5. Tribal court criminal jurisdiction over aliens within the United States has not been addressed by the Supreme Court of the United States. *But see* EBCI v. Torres, 4 Cher. Rep. 9 (2005).

6. Johnson v. M'Intosh, 21 U.S. (8 Wheat.) 543, 589 (1823).

7. Memorandum from Justice Antonin Scalia to Justice William J. Brennan, Jr., regarding Duro v. Reina, 495 U.S. 676 (1998), in Papers of Justice Thurgood Marshall (April 4, 1990) (reproduced from the Collections of the Manuscript Division, Library of Congress).

8. EDWARD HALLETT CARR, WHAT IS HISTORY? 167 (1961).

9. Loftin observes "that there is plenty of academic material that is relevant for the issues of American Indian law but the poor communication between disciplines prevents its application. As a result, legal commentators too often paint a rather inaccurate picture." "The problem, of course, cuts both ways for scholars who lack formal legal training generally fare poorly in legal research." John D. Loftin, *Anglo-American Jurisprudence and the Native American Tribal Quest for Religious Freedom*, 13 AM. INDIAN CULTURE AND RES. J. 1, 33 (1989).

10. JUSTIN B. RICHLAND, ARGUING WITH TRADITION 116 (2008).

11. *Id.* (citations omitted).

12. RICHLAND, *supra* note 10, at 119.

13. *See generally* J. Matthew Martin, *Tribal Courts at a Crossroads*, THE IMPROVEMENT OF THE ADMINISTRATION OF JUSTICE 944–50 (Peter M. Koelling ed., 8th ed. 2016).

14. *See, e.g.*, Ex Parte Crow Dog, 109 U.S. 556 (1883).

15. Robert I. Winner, *The Search for Order, Then and Now*, THE PEN AND PLATE CLUB, February 15, 2018 (copy on file at the Buncombe County Public Library, Asheville, NC).

16. Indeed, Pappas argues it is better understood as an example of "Cherokee *nationalism* outside the context of colonialism." GEORGE D. PAPPAS, THE LITERARY AND LEGAL GENEALOGY OF NATIVE AMERICAN DISPOSSESSION 195 (2017).

17. Loftin, *supra* note 9, at 33 n. 240.

18. *Id.* at 35.

19. William P. Thompson, *Courts of the Cherokee Nation*, 2 CHRON. OF OKLA. 64 (1924).

Appendix

Cherokee Supreme Court Judgment Docket

The infinitive "to transcribe" means literally to make an exact copy of a document or text. I cannot state I have achieved that. This is, however, my best effort to transcribe the Cherokee Supreme Court Judgment Docket. There are others available, and while comparison might have some value, researchers should always start with the original.

I go into detail of the methodological approach to this process in the text. However, an attempt at brevity caused me to leave certain things out. For instance, those who are used to working with manuscript material from this period will understand that the spelling conventions which we take for granted in this century had not reached formal acceptance in the early nineteenth century. Thus, common words are routinely spelled differently, and the names of individuals may differ within the same paragraph. The Cherokee people making these entries may have spoken English as a second language, and no doubt, in some circumstances they were rushed to keep up with the Court. Modern court clerks know exactly what I am talking about. I have attempted, wherever possible, to follow the original. In certain places, I am confident that I know what the unintelligible words are, simply because of the context. I have resisted inserting my speculation in brackets. I have also attempted to follow the format of the manuscript in this transcription, however, the typesetting format for this publication means that cannot be fully reproduced here. Entries in bold typeface indicate the Cherokee Supreme Court struck through that particular language. I have included it for completeness and as an illustration of the Court members' thought processes.

Unquestionably, I made mistakes. However, the goal of this project was not to make a flawless transcription (although as flawless as possible), but rather to have a working transcription in which we can investigate whether this material coheres into stories. I think it does and I hope it works for you.

A Record Book

of

The Proceedings of the Supreme Court of the Cherokee Nation

David McCoy
W. S. Adair
Arch F___

October 9th, 1829

W. S. Adair
David McCoy
Arch Fields

Supreme Court of the Cherokee
Nation, began and held at Newtown.
Thursday the 9th. of October 1823.
Present their Honors John Martin James Daniel
Richard Walker, Circuit Judges James Brown
being absent was chosen for the present term; George
Saunders, Younger, Thomas Saunders, Daniel ____
_______, Terrill Wood

James Crispin Plf	)	Damages ___
vs	)	The Court gives it as their opinion
Nancy West Dft	)	that the defendant shall hold

the contended farm

Court is adjourned until tomorrow 10 O'clock

Friday 10th.

Court convened agreeable to adjournment
Present their Honorable Judges

James Spears Pf	)	Ejectment
vs	)	This case is postponed
Aky Gary Deft	)	untill tomorrow

Court is adjourned until tomorrow 10 O'clock

Saturday 11th.

Court convened agreeable to adjournment
Present their Honors the Jurors
The Court gives it as their opinion for Aky Gary, the
Defendant to keep the place for which James Spears
contends for, the said Aky to pay the said James Spears
ty dollars, and the said Aky is to receive the rent
for which the said Springs wanted the plantation for

Gives from under ____ my hand this 11th
day of October 1823 ____________ CSC {seal}

Kelachlee Plf	)	Plea of debt
vs	)	Dismissed at Kela
William Downing, Jr. Def	)	chlee cost

Court is adjourned until Monday 10 Oclock

Monday 13th.

Court convened agreeable to adjournment
Present their Honors Jurors

John Walker Plf	)	On a plea of defraud
vs	)	It is the opinion of the Court
Joseph Rogers, Dft	)	

that John Walker, jr shall pay Joseph Rogers, def ___
agreeable contract

Court is adjourned until tomorrow 10 Oclock

Tuesday 14th.

Court convened agreeable to adjournment.
Present their Honors. The Jurors

John Langley Pf) On a plea of debt
vs) It is the opinion of the
John Fields Deft) Court that John Fields
shall not pay for a horse that J Langley lays claim
for. William Burgys Ptf)On a plea of debt
vs.)
John Watts Dft) Postponed for tomorrow
W.H. Salmon Ptf)
vs.) The Court gives
Stephins __ John
Wright Dft) It as their opinion
it is to be arbitrated.

New Town 14th October 1823

Being called upon this day by William H.
Salmon and John Wright to arbitrate owners
settled account between Gillispie H. and John
Wright, we are and agreeable to the documents
submitted by Dr. Salmon and the affida
vit of Alexander Kirk one of the surviving copa
___ that John Wright is owing said firm
the amount specified in said a/c and affi
davit to wit one thousand seventy five and
sixty four cents David M_______
True Copy Geo. M __t_z
___ Martin 6.1.6

(As a <u>debt</u> but on examination it was

found their was no claim; nor from any
claiming under me January 26th 1826
Cop. by WS Adair/Alex Kirk)

CJ)

The Court is adjourned untill tomorrow 10 o clock

Wednesday 15th

Court is convened agreeable to adjournment

Present their Honors the Jurors

In cl case submitted to the Court yesterday
W. Burgys vs John Watts ___ the Court gave it

as their opinion that John Watts should pay William
Burgys sixty dollars.

Robert Vann Ptf	)	a plea of debt
	)	It is the opinion of the
vs	)	Court that J. Crutchfield
	)	
Joseph Crutchfield Dft	)	

shall Robert Vann $_20. Recv do 2nd of October 1833. Satisfied

Trustee (the ___ sister Ptf	)	on plea of debt
	)	The Court giving it as
vs	)	their opinion for the said
	)	
Elijah Hicks Dft	)	

Trustee to have the horse appraised and the said E. Hicks
should pay agreeable to the appraising verdict

Telliger Ptf	)	On a plea of debt for a horse
	)	It is the opinion of the Court
vs	)	for Quaty to return the horse
	)	
Quaty, Def	)	

to said Telliger or value thereof
Court is adjourned until tomorrow 10 O clock

Thursday 16th

Court convened agreeable to adjournment
Present their Honors Jurors H D Griffin Foreman

Samuel Carr Pft	)	On a plea of debt
	)	It is the opinion of the
vs	)	Court that Bushy Head
	)	
Bushy Head Def	)	

pay unto Samuel Carr sixty five dollars

Ken Graham Ptf	)	On plea of debt

	)	The Defendants
vs	)	bring notary
	)	
c Avery Vann &		
W. Welch Def	)	

for trial. It is referred to the District Court of Chattoga

James Foster Ptf	)	For a crime of grand
vs.	)	Larceny
	)	Continued
Defoe Vann Decd Adm Dft	)	

Aggy Heopard Ptf	)	On a plea for Damages
	)	It is the opinion of
vs	)	The Court that Cheelio
	)	
Cheelio (of Night) Dft	)	

shall deliver up the contempled farm to A. Heopard
by the 1st day of December next
Court is adjourned until tomorrow 10 Oclock

Friday 17th

Court convened agreeable to adjournment

Present their Honors & Jurors D. Griffin, Fp.

Srucy Vann Ptf	)	On a plea for settlement
	)	
vs	)	
	)	Continued
George Harlin Dft	)	

Young Squirrel Ptf	)	On plea for damages
	)	It is the opinion of the
vs.	)	Court that the Bitor
	)	
The Bitor Dft	)	

Shall pay Young Squirrel eighty dollars.

Court is adjourned until tomorrow 10 O'clock

Saturday 18

Court convened agreeable to adjournment
Present their Honors The Jurors

Joseph Rogers Ptf	)	By the request of the
	)	National Committee, the
vs.	)	Defendant appeals to
	)	
John Walkings Dft	)	

the Court to be holden at this place in October 1824
on a case that the plaintiff obtained against a
defendant on the 14 of October 1823

Court is adjourned until <u>tomorrow</u> Monday 10 O clock

Monday 20

Court convened agreeable to adjournment
Present J. Daniel Richard Walker J. Martin being
absent Court is adjourned until tomorrow 10 O clock

Tuesday 21

Judge Martin being absent Court is adjourned
To Morrow 10 O clock Wednesday 22
Judge Martin being absent Court is adjourned
until tomorrow 10 Oclock

Thursday 23

Court convened agreeable to adjournment
Present their Honors Jurors

Nelly Ragsdale Ptf	)	On a plea of debt
	)	It is the opinion of
vs.	)	the Court the Grier
	)	
The Grier Dft	)	

shelle Nelly Ragsdale sixty dollars.

The Old Ptf	)	On a plea stealing hogs
	)	directed that J Hildz
vs	)	shall pay, the Old, eleven dollars
	)	
John Hildz H○ Dft	)	

Friday 24

Court convened agreeable to adjournment. Present Honors
John Martin, John David, Richard Walker, _________
glg. Jurors George ____, Forman.

Joseph Crutchfield, compromised a judgement, of
obtained, Robert Vause against said Joseph Crutchfield
for $922, witness my hand & seal at this 24th of October 1823
which this is a copy of this proceeding. Martin, CSC

Harry Vicozy Ptf	)	A plea of debt,
	)	
vs	)	This day came the plaintif

	)	
George Lee Dfts	)	and these upon a jury found

George Saunders, Treasurer, upon this acting ____
that the said Harry Vicozy shall recover from the
George Lee, thirt dollars for a horse for which the
light horse took from said Vicozy given
from my hand at New Echota this 24th day October 1823
Martin CSC

Court is adjourned until tomorrow 10 O'Clock

Saturday 25

Court convened agreeable to adjournment. Present
Their Honors The Jurors George Saunders, Foreman
Court is adjourned until 2 O'Clock.

Cherokee Nation	)	Personally came before me John
New Town	)	Martin, one of the Circuit Judges

of the said Nation. Henry Tharpe and after being
duly sworn sayeth on his oath, that about the 20
of September last that a certain Cherokee man
by the name of Terrapin Head traded him a
piece of metal, purporting to be a _________
___ dollars for ___ M ... bearing the date 1802 and
with other markings as a genuine ½ ____ dollar
and on considerations the said piece of metal
is ______ found to be a counterfeit and has been
presented to said Terrapin for redemption The
___ to closure, furthermore this repossessed sayeth
and sworn and subscribed before me this 25 of Oct.
1823 a true copy J. Martin Harry Tharpe

Court is adjourned until the Court is convened

NEW TOWN, Wednesday 20th Octo
1824

The court appointed to be held at this place
cause of Judges being absent court is adjourned
until Monday the 25th

Monday 25

Court convened agreeable to adjournment. Present
Their Honors John Martin, James David, Richard
Walker, Circuit Judges. Jurors George Saunders
Foreman, Thomas Saunders, The Young ___, Daniel
Griffin, The Chip, The Hair Trimmer,

Daniel ___ agent for		
Kerr & Graham Ptfs	)	A plea of
	)	debt
vs.	)	laid over
	)	
Avery Vann & William		
Welch Dfts	)	

Savannah Beck Ptf	)	A plea of debt for an un provi___
	)	It is the opinion of the Court
vs.	)	that J. Terryl shall pay Sees
	)	
John Terryl Dft	)	

vah Beck $200
Court is adjourned until tomorrow at 10 O'clock

Tuesday 26th

Court convened agreeable to adjournment. Present
Their Honors the Jurors George Saunders, Foreman.

Fishing Hawk Ptf	)	On a plea of default
	)	Appeal from __iah Distr
vs.	)	to the Supreme Court

)
William Burgess Dft)
It is the opinion of the Court that William Burgess
shall pay the Fishing Hawk forty dollars for his horse
Court is adjourned until tomorrow 10 O'clock

Wednesday 27th

Court convened agreeable to adjournment. Present
Their Honors The Jurors. G. Saunders, Foreman

Tahsoowottah Ptf) On a appeal from Assoi___
) It is the Opinion of the
vs.) Court that the plaintiff
)
Peter Hellerbrand)
shall pay Peter Hellerbrand eight dollars.

Mary Taylor Ptf) A plea of debt
) It is the Opinion of the
vs) Court for it to be tried
)
Tosc Taylor Dft)
at Craw Fish Town

Archy Doherty Ptf)
)
vs)
)
Jacob Herrsgar Dft) No bill

Court is adjourned until tomorrow 10 O'clock

Thursday 28th

Court convened agreeable to adjournment. Present
Their Honors The Jurors. G. Saunders, Foreman

John Walker, Ptf) on plea of debt

	)	
vs	)	
	)	
Tosc Taylor Dft	)	Corn promised

William Wilson Ptf	)	on a plea of damages sustained
	)	
vs	)	
	)	
Cherokee Nation	)	Nonsuited

Court is adjourned until tomorrow 10 O'clock

Friday 29th

Court convened agreeable to adjournment. Present
Their Honors The Jurors. G. Saunders, Foreman

Water, Ptf	)	
	)	
vs	)	The Jurors give in favor that Shoe
	)	Boots shall keep the Negro he has
Shoe Boots Dft	)	

in possession George Saunders, Foreman

Nancy Griffin Ptf	)	damages sustained
	)	On an appeal from this Court
vs	)	19th of October 1823
	)	
Nancy West Dft	)	

The Jury gives it as their opinion that Nancy West
shall keep the contended farm. G. Saunders, Foreman

Irving Foster Ptf	)	On a plea of debt
	)	
vs	)	It is the opinion of this Court
	)	& Jury that the administrator of
Jesse Vann Dft	)	

Jesse Vann shall pay Irving Foster thirty six dollars
George Saunders, Foreman

Heirs of Graham by their agents. Mcoy	)	A plea of debt
	)	
vs	)	
	)	Verdict for the defendant
William Welch Dft	)	

that the copartnership not being proved

Court is adjourned until tomorrow 10 O'clock

Saturday 30th

Court convened agreeable to adjournment. Present
Their Honors The Jurors. G. Saunders, Foreman

Benjamin Simpson vs. Chowau Ka his old wife

Eliphaling M. Holt, by agent R. Vann Dft	)	On our
	)	
vs	)	appeal
	)	
John Bruge Ptf	)	

It is the Opinion of the Court that EM Holt shall pay
the Plaintiff $230

Court is adjourrned until Monday 10 O'clock

Monday 1 of November

Court convened agreeable to adjournment. Present their
Honors The Jurors. George Saunders, Foreman

Cherokee Nation Ptf	)	For breaking Cherokee law
	)	
vs	)	
	)	

Elisha Dyer Dft	)	No bill

Lewis Ross Ptf	)	Harboring neagros
	)	
vs	)	It is the opinion of
	)	the Court that Rich
Richard & John Ratliff Dfts	)	

ard & John Ratliff shall pay L. Ross $92.00

Josee Rapin Dft	)	
	)	
vs	)	Trespass on property
	)	No bill
John Christie Ptf	)	

Archy Downing Ptf	)	
	)	
vs	)	Appeal from Hickory Log
	)	To National Committee
Archy Downing D	)	Compromized

Court is adjourned until tomorrow 10 O'clock

Tuesday 2nd

Court convened agreeable adjournment. Present their Honors Jurors. George Saunders, Foreman
Court adjourned until tomorrow 10 O'clock

Wednesday 3rd

Court convened agreeable to adjournment. Present their Honors Jurors. George Saunders. Foreman
Court is adjourned until tomorrow 10 O'clock

Thursday 4th

Court convened agreeable to adjournment. Present

their Honors. Jurors. George Saunders. Foreman

The Court gives it as their Order that Judgement be obtained against Jurall Wood for thirty dollars.

Nancy Vann Ptf	)	
	)	A plea for settlement
vs	)	
	)	continued
George Harlan Dft	)	

Court is adjourned until tomorrow 10 O'clock

Friday 5th

Court convened agreeable to adjournment. Present their Honors. Jurors. George Saunders. Foreman

John Hodge wife Ptf	)	
	)	The jury Court giving it as
vs	)	their opinion that Mrs. Hodge
	)	shall lose his horse
Archilla Smith Dft	)	

Court is adjourned until tomorrow 10 O'clock

Saturday 6th

Court convened agreeable to adjournment. Present their Honors. Jurors. George Saunders, Foreman

Ordered by the Supreme Court that Richard Ross be summoned to appear at this place the second Monday in October next to answer to a complaint that Sarah Hughes and others has obtained from the National Committee.

Court is adjourned until Monday 8th

Monday 8th

Court convened agreeable to adjournment. Present
their Honors. Jurors. George Saunders, Foreman

Court is adjourned until tomorrow 10 O'clock

Tuesday 9th

Court convened agreeable to adjournment. Present
their Honors. Jurors. George Saunders, Foreman

Court is adjourned until tomorrow 10 O'clock

Wednesday 10th

Court convened agreeable to adjournment. Present
their Honors. Jurors. George Saunders, Foreman
Wahachee absent.

Benjamin Simpson Ptf)
)
vs)
)
Chuaukee his old wife Dft) Continued

Court is adjourned until evening

Court convened agreeable to adjournment. Present
Court is adjourned until tomorrow 10 O'clock

Thursday 11th

Court convened agreeable to adjournment. Present
their Honors. Geo Saunders, Foreman
Wahachee absent.

Court is adjourned until the second Monday in
October next

New Town October 10th 1825

Court did not convene agreeable to adjournment

Tuesday 11th

Some of the Court being absent Can't form a quorum

Wednesday 12

Thursday 13

Court convened agreeable to adjournment from the 11th of November last. Present their Honors John Martin, James Daniel, Richard Walker, and James Brown, Circuit Judges, Jurors Daniel Griffin Foreman, Thomas Saunders, The Chip, Suttoowakee George Saunders, Deer in the Water, Wahachee being absent, Court is adjourned until tomor row 10 O'clock

Friday 14th

Court convened agreeable to adjournment Present Their Honors John Martin & part of the Jurors being absent, Court is adjourned until tomor row 10 O'clock

Saturday 15th

Court convened agreeable to adjournment Present Their Honors & Part of the jurors being absent. Court adjourned until Monday 10 O'clock

Monday 17th

Court convened agreeable to adjournment Present their Honors John Martin & Jurors

George Saunders Foreman, Daniel Griffin, Thos
Saunders, The Chip, Suttoowakee

Johnson Fields Ptf	)	
	)	a plea of debt
vs	)	Judgment in favor of
	)	The plaintiff with cost of debt
Mathew Hicks Dft	)	$22

Oocoosee Ptf	)	
	)	a plea of trespass
vs	)	It is the opinion of the Court
	)	That the defendant shall
Crying Wolf Dft	)	

keep the contended mare George Saunders Fore

Benjamin Simpson Ptf	)	
	)	
vs	)	
	)	
Chuaukee his old wife Dft	)	Continued

Court is adjourned until tomorrow 10 O'clock

Tuesday 18th

Court convened agreeable to adjournment Present
Their Honors John Martin & Geo Saunders Fore

Thomas Petit Ptf	)	A plea for settlement
	)	Nonsuited with costs of
vs	)	suit. G. Saunders Foreman
	)	
John Downing Dft	)	

suit Whirl Wind for six days attending at
50 Cents per day as a witness $3.00

Mary Taylor Ptf) a plea of debt
) It is the opinion of the
vs) Court that Mary Taylor
)
Fox Taylor Dft)
shall have half the price the negroe was
sold for, say $400.00

George W. Smool Ptf) a plea for a horse
) It is the opinion of the
vs) Court that the plaintiff
)
Joseph Phillips Dft)
shall recover his horse, saddle & bridle that the
defendant bought of W. Wilkinson

Thomas Chissom &)
R. Ratliff Ptfs) a plea for
)
vs) Negroes
)
Ivy Path Killer & Heirs Dft) Continued

Court is adjourned until tomorrow 10 O'clock

Wednesday 19th

Court convened agreeable to adjournment
Present their Honors John Martin & Geo Foreman

Sally Hughes Ptf) a plea for negroes
)
vs)
)
Richard Roe Dft) Continued

Nelson & John Riley Ptfs)

	)	
vs	)	
	)	
Samuel Gunter & J Brown	)	Continued
Heirs of R. Riley Dec Dfts	)	Continued

Ivy Pathkiller)
& Heirs)

The Judges of the Supreme Court have decided
that they have no cognisence of the above case
from circumstances & evidences introduced in
the above case, it did not concurred the cons
titution Act J Martin CJ

Court is adjourned until tomorrow 10 Oclock

Thursday, 20th

Court convened agreeable to adjournment Present
their Honors John. Martin and the Jurors G. Saunders Fore

On motion it is ordered that the proceedings against
Richard & John Ratliff wherein Lewis Rob ws
plaintiff against Richard & John Ratliff Dfts
be stopped until further directed
It is the opinion of the Court that Richard
Rowe shall hold the negroes that Sarah Hughes
and others contended for,
Court is adjourned until tomorrow 10 O'clock

Friday, 21st

Court convened agreeable to adjournment Present
their Honors John. Martin and the Jurors G. Saunders Fore

Archy Foreman Ptf	)	For breaking the Cherokee Law
	)	Judgment confessed $10.00

vs	)	with cost of suit $4.50
	)	
Richard Huffacre Dft	)	

Cherokee Nation Ptf	)	Indictment for murder of
	)	Ezthral Wright, kingstick's
vs	)	brother, We the Judges of
	)	
Gahcowe Dft	)	

the Supreme Court find no bill against the Dft Gahcowe, given from under my hand at New Town this 21st of October 1825 J Martin CS C

Jesse Bushy Head Ptf	)	For breaking the Cherokee
	)	for selling spiritous liquors
vs	)	
	)	It is the opinion of the jury
Samuel Henry Dft	)	

that Samuel Henry has violated the Cherokee Law & be fined $100 George Saunders, Foreman

Court is adjourned until tomorrow 10 O'clock

Saturday, 22nd

Court convened agreeable to adjournment Present their Honors John. Martin and Jurors G. Saunders For Judge James Brown being absent

George Harlan Ptf	)	A plea for settlement
	)	
vs	)	
	)	Continued
Nancy Talley Dft	)	

Court is adjourned until Monday 24th at 10 O'clock

Monday 24

Court convened agreeable to adjournment
Present their Honors John. Martin &
Jurors George Saunders. Foreman

Nancy Miller Ptf	)	A plea for horses
	)	
vs	)	
	)	
Jefsee E Bean Dft	)	Continued
Belsoy Connor Ptf	)	A plea for a marl gar
	)	
vs	)	
	)	
Culsowe & others Dfts	)	Continued
Sally West Ptf	)	The right for a negro
	)	girl & used thereto
vs	)	
	)	
John Walker Son Dft	)	Continued
Thomas Fields Ptf	)	Violating the Cherokee Law
	)	
vs	)	
	)	It is the opinion of the Court
John Miller Dft	)	that the defendant be fined
	)	$5.00
Thomas Fields Ptf	)	Violating the
	)	Cherokee Law
vs	)	
	)	
John Miller Dft	)	Acquitted

Court is adjourned until tomorrow 10 O'Clock

Present their Honors J. Martin & Jurors G. Saunders

Tuesday 25

Court convened agreeable to adjournment
Present their Honors J. Martin & Jurors &

Susanna Otter ___ Ptf	)	A plea of debt
	)	
vs	)	
	)	
Jesse E Bean Dft	)	Continued
Jacob Seabott Ptf	)	appeal from from
	)	Amoiah District
vs	)	
	)	
Taylor Eldridge Dft	)	Continued
Archy Foreman Ptf	)	Violating the Cherokee Law
	)	
vs	)	
	)	
William Blythe Dft	)	Continued
Betsy Walker Ptf	)	A plea of debt
	)	
vs	)	
	)	
William Blythe Dft	)	Continued to 1826
Wif & Seunnataye Ptf	)	Continued
	)	
vs	)	
	)	
George Hicks Dft	)	
___ Jacks wife Ptf	)	
	)	

vs	)	
	)	
Young Squirrel	)	Continued
Jesse Bushy Head Ptf	)	Right for a Negroe
	)	
vs	)	
	)	
Polly Rain Crow Dft	)	Continued
The Leaper & Co. Ptf	)	
	)	
vs	)	
	)	
Polly Lovit Dft	)	Continued
Nathaniel Peake Ptf	)	
	)	
vs	)	
	)	
Cheanankaah Dft	)	Continued
Jackson & McConnell Ptfs	)	Appeal from Amora
	)	
vs	)	
	)	
Bridge Maker & Wife Dfts	)	Continued

The Court recognize the will of Samuel Riley deceased, to be his last will and testament as authenticated by the deposition of R. Richards Phisicien, who attended on said Sam Riley Dec. a in his last sickness, given from under my hand at New Town this 25th of October 1825

J. Martin C.S.C.

Court is adjourned until tomorrow 10 O'Clock

Wednesday 26th

Court convened agreeable to adjournment
Present their Honors J. Martin & Jurors G. Saunders Foreman

Thomas Fields Ptf	)	violation of the Cherokee law
	)	
vs	)	
	)	
Cyrus _____ Dft	)	No Bill

John Spears Ptf	)	Appeal from Anoiahdis
	)	
vs	)	
	)	
The Horse Fly Dft	)	A judgement in favor of Horse

Fly

It is ordered by the Court having the consent Sally West Ptf and John Walker Son Dft be submitted to arbitration on the present instance to be composed of the following persons, to wit John Loury, ___ McCoy, Joseph Vann, Walter Adiar, Thos. Wilson & Richard Fields and their decision to be final and conclusive accord ing to law, New Town 25 October 1825
J Martin, C.S.C.

It is the opinion of the jury from evidence produced that William Blythe did not violate the Cherokee law.

Ordered by the Honorable Supreme Court that the case submitted to arbitration between Teresa West Ptf and John Walker son. Dft. be postponed until the second Monday in October 1826

It is the opinion of the jury that Nancy Talley shall pay George Harlan for the Negroe to wit, Harry, he contends for, the said negroe to be a valued by two or three disinterested persons .... Cherokee Nation

Katy Harlan (widow) comes in person before the Judges of Supreme Court and declares that if she has ever previous to this date made a will or gave to any person a power to transact her business the same is hereby revoked and of no effect signed in the presence of the Court this 26 of October 1825 John Martin, CJ, James Daniel, CJ

Katy her X mark Harlan

It is the opinion of the jury that ________ shall keep the horses that Betsy Walker contended for with costs of suit. G. Saunders, Foreman

Court is adjourned until Tomorrow 10 O'Clock

Thursday 27th

Court convened agreeable to adjournment
Present their Honors J. Martin & Jurors G. Saunders

To all whom these presents shall come, know that I Katy Harlan, a citizen of the Cherokee Nation, on account of the Natural Love affection which I have and feel towards my affectionate daughter Sarah Westall valued for devises other good causes & considerations use wherein, to moving do by these presents give and of my own free will record surrender up to her the said Sarah Westall my right title and claim, which I have to a Negroe woman named Quate and her two children Lose and Suse, the right of which said Negroes descended to me, as the lawful heir of my beloved brother Five Killer Dec.d in ____ money whereof I hereunto set my hand & seal {seal} this 27th day of October 1825. Katy her X mark Harlan

Ordered by the Honorable the Supreme Court
that Bushyhead shall have another hearing
wherein Samuel Carr is plaintiff and
Bushy Head Defendant in the Supreme Court
1826.

It is the opinion of the jury that Polly Rain
Crow shall hold the negroe Jesse Bushy
Head contended for, G. Saunders, Foreman.

Court is adjourned until tomorrow 10 O'Clock

Friday 28th

Court convened agreeable to adjournment
Present their Honors John Martin The Jurors G. Saunders

It is the opinion of the jury that the Rattling
Gourd shall hold the contended share that
Archy Fields contends for, on the McKayack
road, George Saunders, Foreman

We the Jury find that Jesse E. Bean is
fined by default to pay Susannah Otter ___
one hundred & two dollars for the farm said
Bean bought of said Susannah with costs of
judgment against Jesse E. Bean Dft
By Default. Whereas Nancy Miller was Plaintiff
with costs of suit.

Court is adjourned until tomorrow 10 O'clock.

Saturday 29th

Court convened agreeable to adjournment.
Present their Honors John Martin & Jurors G. Saunders

Bets Brown Ptf vs John Walkerson Dft

vs
We the jury find by proofs that was produced
that George Hicks shall hold the _______ that
Mrs. Suntoye contended for. G. Saunders, Foreman

Court is adjourned until Monday 31st 10 O'Clock

Monday 31st

Court convened agreeable to adjournment.
Present their Honors John Martin & Jurors G. Saunders, Fore

Widow Skinka Ptf)
)
vs)
)
Wolley her stepdaughter Dft)

It is the opinion of the Jury that the Young Squirrel
shall hold the property that Quakah ___ wife
contends for with costs of suit. G. Saunders, Foreman

It is the opinion of the Jury that Cheananna
shall have sails split and have a place cleared the
same size that she claims of William Reed, with
costs of suit. George Saunders, Foreman

It is the opinion of the Jury that the Leaper __
is justifiable in his proceedings with Polly Lovit
George Saunders, Foreman

Court is adjourned until tomorrow 10 O'Clock.

Tuesday, 1st of November

Court convened agreeable to adjournment.
Present their Honors John Martin & Jurors G. Saunders, Fore

It is the opinion of the Jury that John Walkerson shall pay Betsy Brown for her negroe. G. Saunders, Fore.

Judgment in favor of Jackson & McConnell against Bridge Maker and Wife by default $19,, 12½

Judgment against Taylor Eldridge and William Blythe in favor of Jacob Seabolt, be default $51.73

Judgment in favor of Horsefly against John Spears by default

Court is adjourned until tomorrow 10 O'Clock

Wednesday 2nd

Court convened agreeable to adjournment.
Present their Honors John Martin & Jurors G. Saunders

J____ Talley Ptf	)	It is the opinion of the Court
	)	That Archy Downing shall
vs	)	pay J. Talley a horse of equal
	)	
Archy Downing Dft	)	

value for the one taken to be valued by two disinterested men.

Archy Foreman vs. The Horsefly, for the right of a horse is put off until October Court 1826

Court is adjourned until tomorrow 10 O'Clock

Thursday 3d

Court convened agreeable to adjournment.
Present their Honors John Martin & G. Saunders, Foreman

Archy Foreman Ptf	)	Contends for the right
	)	of a horse which is

vs	)	
	)	
Horsefly Dft	)	

put off until October Court, 1826

Peacock Ptf	)	It is ordered for
	)	it to be tried at
vs	)	Hightower District
	)	
James Foster Dft	)	

Susannah Otter Lifton Ptf	)	Judgment
	)	in favor of the
vs	)	Plaintiff
	)	
Jesse E. Bean	)	

This is to certify that Joseph Vann
attended as witness nineteen days
wherein Susannah Otter Lipton was Plaintiff &
Jesse E. Bean Defendant 30 cents per day
___ $9.30 It is ordered by the Honorable the
Supreme Court of the Cherokee Nation for this
to be collected
Court is adjourned until the second Monday in October.

<u>October & November Term, 1826</u>

Friday, 20th Oct. 1826

The Court met

Present:

Their Honors	John Martin James Brown W.S. Adair James Daniel

John Hill vs Wm. Kuave	)))))	The Court finds for the Plaintiff John Hill ___ fifty dollars & costs of suit.

The Court adjourned until 10 O'Clock tomorrow

Saturday, 21st

The court met according to adjournment

Present their Honors Judges John Martin, James Brown, W.S. Adiar and James Daniel—

The Cherokee Nation vs David Quinton, Sr	)))))	charge with horse stealing

The Court acquitted the Dft of the above charg

Court is adjourned until tomorrow 10 O'Clock

<u>October & November 1826</u>

The Court met according to adjournment
Present J. Martin, James Brown,
W.S. Adair & J. Daniel Judges—

The Court adjourned until tomorrow 10 O'Clock

Tuesday 24th

The Court met according to adjournment
Present J. Martin, J. Brown, W.S. Adair
& Jam. Daniel

Jno. Woodard	)	
	)	The Court find for the deft
vs	)	
	)	Cost of appeal $1.20
Archy Murphese	)	

Edley Thingston	)	The Court find for the
	)	heirs & widow of Edward
vs	)	Thingston, dece. The plantation
	)	
James Tourneau	)	

or improvements on which they now live.

The Court adjourned until tomorrow 10 O'Clock.

Wednesday 25

The met agreeable to agreeable to adjournment
Present J. Martin, J. Brown, W.S. Adair &
James Daniel

October and November 1826

Wednesday 25th Oct.

John Sheppard & others	)	
heirs of Bitey Springstow	)	Try the right of two
dec	)	negros namely, Fillis &
vs	)	Darky—
	)	
David McNair &	)	
his wife Delilah	)	

The Court decide a follows. The wench
Fillis in the first purchased was the property
of William Burgis serv. Bitey Springstow
& Delilah McNair, and after the purchase
it does not appear from any witness
that the old man Burgis had any
interest in the negro woman Fillis but
that the right appears to have been
in Bitey Springstow after giving to
Delilah McNair the child Darky for
part of the property paid in for this
purchase of the old wench Fillis, and
as the right of the Fillis is in Bitey
Springstow, the old woman Burgis &
William Burgis had no right to sell
her except any interest they had
in the said nigro woman——and
the Court find for the Plaintiffs
Edward Adair, John Shepard, Polly
Springstow & James Vann against the
Defendants David & Delilah McNair
two hundred & sixty six dollar & sixty
six cents & costs of suit—
costs of appeal $15.96 to C.R. Hicks, Treasurer
Court is adjourned until tomorrow 10 O'Clock

Execution is signed
3rd November 1826

October and November 1826

Thursday 26th

The Court met according to adjournment

Mary Taylor Ptf	)	The Court find for the
	)	Ptf thirty dollars and

vs	)	costs of suit $1-80
	)	
Thos. Feilds & Co. Dft	)	

Taylor Eldridge Ptf	)	The Court find for
	)	the plaintiff 51"/56in
vs	)	
	)	
John Walking Dft	)	

and costs of Suit. Cost appeal $3.10½
Execution issued 12 Nov 1826
Re: The above cost of three dollars 10½ 2nd Nov. John Martin SC

Court is adjourned until tomorrow 9 O'Clock

Friday 27th

The Court met according to adjournment Present Le

Archy Downing Ptf	)	The Court find for
	)	the defendant
vs	)	
	)	
Charles Vance Dft	)	

Costs of the appeal $1.80

James Hughs Ptf	)	To recover part feery on
	)	Coosa River
vs	)	
	)	
Path Killer Dft	)	

The Court decides that James Hughes the plaintff is equally interested in the ferry as the defendant

Court is adjourned until tomorrow 9 O'Clock

Saturday 28th

Court met agreeable to adjournment Present
John Martin Judges Walter S. Adair J. Daniel

October and November

Saturday 28th

Court met agreeable to adjournment Present John Martin, James Brown, Walter S. Adair & J Daniel

Charles R. Hicks Ptf	)	Slander for the wrong
	)	of robbery or stealing
vs	)	
	)	
James Brown	)	
William Williams	)	
Jenny Williams Dfts	)	

The Court decides that the charges alleged against the plaintiff for the above offences has not been proven and that there is no thing purporting in the instructions given by Charles R. Hicks to a certain company of men appertaining to theft or robbery and that the plaintiff is honorably acquitted of such charges

J Martin C.S.C.

Cherokee Nation	)	
	)	No prosecutor
vs	)	
	)	
Edward Crittinton	)	Dismissed
Taluskee	)	

Michael Heldebrand Ptf	)	Court find for the
	)	Defendant
vs	)	
	)	

Sleeping Rabbit & Son Dft)

Monday 30

The Court met according to adjournment
Present John
Martin, James Brown,
Walter S. Adair & Jos. Daniel
Judges—

Ruth Willsone	)	Try right of a gray horse
	)	The Court find for the Ptff
vs	)	Thirty dollars & Costs of suit
	)	
Bark Foreman	)	

Execution issued 3d November 1826

October & November Term 1826

The Court adjourned until Tomorrow

Tuesday 31st October

The Court met according to adjournment
Present Their Honors, John Martyn
James Daniel, Jas. Brown, Walter S. Adair

Eliza Ratliff	)	Recover for house burning
	)	The court find for the plaintiff
	)	forty five dollars & seventy five
Lolly Robinson	)	cents & costs of suit

Costs of appeal $2.75 cts

Arch. Fields	)	Recover for cattle
	)	The Court find
	)	for the defendants—
	)	
W. Williams &	)	
Jane Williams	)	

Witnesses	Henry Frishower	7 days—$5.25
	Amy Wolf	7 days—5.25
	Ben. Avery	17 days—12.00

The Court adjourned until tomorrow 10 O'Clock

Wednesday 1st Nov. 1826

The Court met according to adjournment
Present their Honors, John Martin, Jas.
Daniel, Jos. Brown & Walter S. Adair

Sarah West	)	Try rights for a negro woman
	)	Quaity & her two children
vs	)	The Court decide that Mrs. West
	)	is entitled to the negro woman
Jno. Walker v	)	Quaity only.—
	)	
&	)	
	)	
Katy Five Killer	)	

November 2nd 1826

The Court adjourned until Tomorrow

Thursday 2nd

The Court met agreeable to adjournment
Present Judges Jno Martin, James Daniel
James Brown & W.S. Adair

Friday 3rd Nov

The Court met according to adjournment
Present Judges John Martin, James Daniel, James Brown & W.S. Adair

Cherokee Nation vs Elijah Hicks	)))))	Purchasing spiritous liquor from a Citizen of the U. States

The Court decide that the defendant
is guilty of the breach of the Cherokee Law—

The Court adjourned until tomorrow

Saturday 4th Nov

The Court met according to
adjournment
Present Jno Martin, James Brown
James Daniel & W.S. Adair Judges—

No business appearing on the
docket. The Court adjourned to
Monday 10 O'Clock
October & Nov. Term 1826

Monday 4th (Sic) Nov.

The Court met according to adjournment
Present Judges John
Martin, James Daniel James Brown,
& W.S. Adair—

No business appearing in Court this Court adjourned to tomorrow 10 O'Clock

Tuesday 7th Nov.

The Court met according to adjournment
Present John Martin,
James Brown, James Daniel
and Walter S. Adair Judges—

Ja, Ra, Tul, La	)	Recover for a black horse said to be stolen
	)	
vs	)	
	)	
Wha. Ya, Hut, Ta	)	

The Court find for the defendant Wah, Ya, Hut, Ta.—

The Court adjourned to Tomorrow 10 O'Clock

<u>October & Nov. Term 1826</u>

<u>Wednesday 8th Nov.</u>

The Court met according to adjournment
Present Judges Martin, Daniel
Brown & Adair

No business appearing before Court
The Court adjourned until the Second
Monday October next.

<u>October & November Term</u>

<u>Tuesday 16</u>

The Court met according to
adjournment
Present John Martin, James Brown
Richard Walker & Walter
S. Adair Judges—

Joseph Woffard	)	Damages: Salt & Bath
	)	The Court find for the

vs	)	Defendant & tax the ___ (ptf?)
	)	with the costs—
Laura Wood	)	

Witnesses—	John Hite	5 days—$3.75
	William Doroning	5 do—3.75
	Tho. Pitet Sr.—	5 do—3.75
	Tho. Pitet Jr.—	10 do—7.50
Cost of appeal on $25.00—		1.50
		$20.25

Cherokee Nation ptf	)	The Court find for the defendant
	)	
vs	)	
	)	
Brice Martin Dft	)	

Court is adjourned until tomorrow 10 O'Clock

Wednesday 17th

Court convened agreeable to adjournment Present

October & November 1827

Wednesday 17th

Owl Sowce	)	Debt.
	)	
vs	)	
	)	
Jesse Leon	)	The Court find for the

Plaintiff twenty eight
dollars & Cost of Suit

Cost of appeal	——	$1.68
Witness—The Day 13 days		9.75
		Cost **$11.43**

22 of October 1827 Rec. Of the defendant one dollar & sixty eight cents cost for appeal. John Martin	)	S.J.
Joshua Buffington & Alfred Hudson Heirs of J. Buffington, Dec.d vs Moses Downing Heir of J. Downing, Dec.d	)	Trover Try the rights of a certain Negro Boy Jack

Court find for the defendant and tax the plaintiffs with the Costs

Cost of appeal on $250.00 Paid		$15.00
Witnesses	Thomas Petit	8 days—6.00
	John Wright	7 do—5.25
	Wm. Reid	11 do—8.25
	Tuckqua	3 do—2.25
		$31.75

Rec the same costs of fifteen dollar 2nd Nov. 1829
John Martin S.J.

The Court adjourned until 10 O'Clock

October & November Term 1827

Thursday 18th

The met according to adjournment

Recd of the Supreme Court an Execution against Elijah Hicks where the Cherokee Nation is plaintiff for one hundred dollars principal

and six dollars cost of appeal
18th Oct. 1827—George Hicks
Marsh C.D.

Joseph Vann	)	
	)	The Court find for the plaintiff
vs	)	sixty dollars with Costs of suit
	)	
Alexander Saunders	)	

Cost of appeal a— $3.60
Rec'd 19th Oct. 1827 of the Defendant three dollars & sixty cents in full on this day the xxxx nation in this above case John Martin

Court is adjourned until Tomorrow 10 O'Clock

Friday 19th

Court met according to adjournment Present

Saturday 20th

Court met according adjournment Present Their Honors

Cherokee Nation	)	The Court find the prisoner
	)	guilty, his sentence to receive
vs	)	ten lashes on his bare back
	)	
Jesse Ratley Dft	)	

William Burns 10 days	$8.20
John Brown 15 days	11.25
Greenberry Perdue 10 days	8.25

Peggy Path Killer	)	The Court find for
	)	the plaintiff two hundred
vs	)	& four dollars and
	)	

Path Killer Pl Chief)
Cost of Suit $12.24

The Court adjourned until Monday 10 O'Clock

Monday 22nd

The Court convened agreeable to adjournment Present

George M. Walters	)	Trover, by the right of a certain
	)	negroe fellow named Peter
vs	)	The Court find for the Plaintiff
	)	
The Swimmer & R Scott	)	

	The Per Costs on the appeal		$24.00
Witnesses	Joseph Holland	10 days at 75 Cents	$7.50
	Samuel Talley	de %	4.50
			$36.00

Monday 22nd October 1827

John Downing	)	Trover, by the right of a
	)	certain negroe woman Miley
vs	)	The Court find for the plaintiff
	)	
Martin Downing & mother	)	

	The per Cost for the appeal	$24.00
Witnesses	James Cullington attended 12 days	9.00
	Alexander Saunders 3 days	2.25
	Harry Downing 12 "	9.00
	William Reid 14 %	10.50
		$54.75

Execution issued 22nd
October 1829

Court is adjourned until tomorrow 10 O'Clock

Tuesday 23rd

Court convened agreeable to adjournment Present

Cherokee Nation vs John Fields	)	Fellony The Court decide that the defendant pay to the Nation three dollars, considered to be the percent due, & two dollars to the plaintiff for damages 23rd of October 1827
Walter Adair vs George Hicks	)	Damages Mistrial 23rd October 1827
Cherokee Nation vs Bledsoe Gore	)	Fellony Charge for stealing a (**The Court adjourns until 10'Oclock tomorrow**) The Court acquit the defendant of the charge
Betsy Walker vs William Blythe	)	Debt on Contract The Court find for the Plaintiff $32.00 23rd October 1827

	Percent on Appeal	$1.92
Witnesses	Jesse Scott attended 24 days @ 75	18
	George Fields do 14 % 75	10.50
		$30.42

Tuesday 23 October 1827

Thomas Woodard	)	Case for non compliance of duty
	)	
vs	)	
	)	
John Walker, Marshal	)	

Court find for the plaintiff twenty six dollars

Per Cent on appeal			$9.50
Witnesses	Ezekiel Fields attended 28 days @ 75 per		$21.00
	H___ Ralley do 10 do		7.50
	Jesse Scott do 10 do		7.50
	Saml. McDaniel do	26 do	9.50
		________	$83.06
			"6

Court is adjourned until tomorrow 10 O'Clock

Wednesday 24th

Court met according to adjournment Present

Watty Fields	)	Trover, for a certain cow
	)	
vs	)	
	)	
Big Cabin	)	The Court find for the Plaintiff

Cost of Appeal		$–.60
Witnesses	The Waggon 11 days at 75 Cents per day	$8.25
	Tekunneskee 8 da	6.00
	The Woman 11 da	8.25

Satisfied and execution returned by

Jos M Lynch Ct Marshal May 15, 1829

Peter Helebrand	)	Debt on contract	
	)		
vs	)	The Court find against the	
	)	defendant Taloneskee alone	
	)	for fifty dollars	
Cullonouske &	)		
Taloneskee	)		
Cost of Appeal			$3.00
	Young Wolf 16 days		12.00

<u>October Term 1827</u>

Wednesday 24th Brot over	$15.00
Witness Peggy Morgan attended 22 days	$16.50

Betsy Walker	)	Debt for Ostrich Feathers	
	)		
vs	)	The Court find for the defendant	
	)	24th October, 1827	
Chekayoue	)		
Percent on appeal			$1.27

Betsy Springston	)	Damages for a horse	
	)		
vs	)	The Court find for the defendant	
	)	21	
John Walking	)		

Percent on appeal		2.40
Witnesses	James Forman attended 5 days Paid	$3.75
	John Sheppard da 4 da	3.00
	Edward Adair da 4 da	3"00
	Richard Foreman da	
	Richard Foremans wife da 2 da	2.50
	Tahcheche da 1 da	"75
	Bend Abott da 1 da	75

Henry Abott 1 75

Court is adjourned until tomorrow 9 O'Clock

<u>October Term 1827</u>

Thursday 25

Court met according tomorrow to adjournment
Present

James P. Chisholm and others vs vs	)	Damage to recover a ferry
Alex McCoy	)	

As the Committee & Council have had the matter of controversy under their considerations and never legally decided the rights of the landing contended for, we therefore are opinion that the rights of establishing, Roads, ferry's & turnpikes is not visited in the Courts, but that the only authority must come from the Committee & Council and therefore cant establish the ferry to be rightfully possession in either party—and decide that each party has their own costs

Court is adjourned until tomorrow 10 O'Clock

Friday 26th

Court convened agreeable adjournment Present

Peggy Morgan	)	Damages for glass ware $50.00
vs	)	
Archd Foreman	)	The Court find for the defendants 26th Oct.o 1827

Joseph Shears)

Percent on appeal	Paid	$3.00
Witnesses	Isaac Bushy Head attended 9 days	6.75
	Jesse Bushy Head do 9	6.75
	John Walker no 9	6.75

Rcd of Peggy Morgan three dollars in full of all Cost of appeal in the above case. 27th Oct. 1827 John Martin SCJ

October Term 1827

Friday 26th

Richard Fields)
&)
Nathan Hicks)
)
vs)
)
John Ross)

From the Opinion of the Circuit Judges

The Court decide that the Courts of Justice have cognisance of cases transpiring as far back as the year one thousand and eight hundred. 1800—

Court is adjourned until tomorrow 9 O'Clock

Saturday 27th

Court met according to adjournment Present

Court is adjourned until Monday 10 O'Clock

Monday 29th

Court convened agreeable to adjournment Present

James Foster	)	Recovery of stolen cattle
	)	
vs	)	
	)	The Court find for Plaintiff
The Peacock Exec	)	sixteen dollars
of Jesse Vann Decd	)	

Percent on appeal		$ 96
Witnesses	Nicowce attended 9 days	$6.75
	Ocunnah ad 9 days	6.75

<u>Monday 29 October 1827</u>

James Foreman	)	Debt on Note
	)	
vs	)	Judgment for the plaintiff for
	)	Forty dollars 29th October 1827
Necootiah	)	

Percent on appeal	$2-40
Wit Richard Foreman attended 17 days	12"75

Flose Taylor	)	Debt
	)	
vs	)	
	)	
Caty McEntosh	)	Judgment in favor of the

Plaintiff for two dollars & 40 cents which is the cost of appeal—
Recd of the defendant two dollars & forty cents in full of the appeal in the above case

John Martin S.J.

Gidian Childers	)	Debt
	)	

vs	)	
	)	
John Walker Sr	)	Judgment against the

Plaintiff

Cost of appeal ________________________________ $0.60
Recd the above cost of sixty cents
John Martin S.J.

Execution issued on 22 Dec 1832

Thigh Walker	)	Debt
	)	
vs	)	The Court find the plaintiff fifty
	)	seven bushels of corn or
Robert Fields	)	seventeen dollars

The per cent on appeal, cost of appeal $1.14
Recd the above cost of one dollar & 14 cts. John Martin S.J

Court is adjourned until tomorrow 9 O'Clock

Tuesday 30th October 1827
Court met agreeable to adjournment Present.

Court is adjourned until tomorrow 9 O'Clock

Wednesday 31st

Court met agreeable to adjournment Present.

Court is adjourned until tomorrow 9 O'Clock

Thursday 1st November

Court met according to adjournment Present

William Boling	)	debt on a Note
	)	Judgment by default against

vs	)	the defendants for thirteen
	)	
___ & Kisukanah	)	

dollars. Percent on appeal $ 78'

Court is adjourned until tomorrow 9 O'Clock

Friday 2nd Nov.

Court met agreeable to adjournment Present

John Walking	)	Debt to recover costs ___
	)	Judgment for the plaintiff thirty
vs	)	nine dollars & sixty & half cents
	)	
Jacob Seabolt	)	

2nd of Nov. 1827

Court is adjourned until tomorrow 9 O'Clock

Saturday 3rd of Nov.

Court is adjourned until the second Monday in October 1828

<u>October & November Term 1828</u>

<u>Friday 24th</u>

The Court met and formed a quorum. Present Andrew Ross, John Huss, and Walter S. Adair Judges—

The Court have duly elected Elijah Hicks Clerk of said Court

The Cherokee Nation	)	<u>Wolf Prosecutor</u>)

	)	Charged with stealing money
vs	)	The Court acquits the defendants
	)	
Robert Saunders	)	
& Wayahuttah	)	

The Nation	)	Stealing
Chu, wo, Rul, lev pro	)	Court find the dft
	)	Beaver Carrier guilty
vs	)	and sentence him to seventy
	)	five lashes
Beaver Carrier	)	

And give judgment in favor of the prosecutor
for ten dollars & Costs.
Witnesses
The Fencir 14 days $10.50

The Court adjourned til 10 O'Clock Tommorrow—

<u>October Term 1828</u>

<u>Saturday 25th</u>

The Court met according to adjournment
Present Andrew Ross, John Huss and
Walter S. Adair. Judges

The Court adjourned to Monday
10 O'Clock a.m.

Court convened according to adjournment
Present the Honorable Judges Monday October 27th

Court adjourned to Tuesday
Morning

The Court met according to adjournment
Present the Honorable Judges 28th

William Berrt	)	To recover the price of a
by his agent	)	horse
James Gibson	)	The Court finds a bill for
	)	the pltf. The sum of
vs	)	one hundred & fifteen dollars
	)	
William Lastley	)	

Cost of appeal—$6.90 Stay taken on the above judgment according to law

Andrew Ross
James X Lastley
His Mark

Execution issued 20th August 1829
for the costs

Witness Elijah Hicks, CK, S.C.
The principal paid by Wm Lastley
July 13, 1829

October Term 1828

Tuesday 28th

The Nation	)	Horse stealing—
	)	In this case the prisoner
vs	)	pleads Guilty and the Court
	)	sentences him
John C. Bird	)	the said John C. Bird to

receive one hundred lashes
on the bare back

Court is adjourned to 10 O'Clock tomorrow.

Wednesday 29th

The Court met according to adjournment.

Present A Ross, John Huss and Walter S. Adair, Judges

Court is adjourned until 10 O'Clock tomorrow.

Thursday 30th Oct

The Court met according to adjournment.
Present Andrew Ross, John Huss & Walter S. Adair Judges

Court is adjourned to 10 O'Clock tomorrow A.M.

Friday Oct. 31st

Court met according to adjournment.
Present the Honorable Judges—

Walter Adair	)	An action for collecting
	)	unlawful fees
vs	)	The Court finds a verdict
	)	for the defendant
George Hicks	)	

Archullach Smith	)	An action for
	)	a horse
vs	)	The Court finds
	)	for the defendant
Andrew Ross	)	and costs for the Plaintiffs

Witnesses
Goose————————$9.75
Patin————————3.00
Pigeon———————3.00
Young Hogg————
Rede——————————

Court is adjourned to 10 O'Clock tomorrow morning.

Saturday Morning Nov 1st

Court convened according to adjournment Present the Honorable Judges

Court adjourned until 10 O'Clock Monday

Monday Nov. 3rd

Court met according to adjournment
Present the hbl judges

Court adjourned until Tuesday morning 10 O'clock

Tuesday morning 4th Nov.

Court met according to adjournment
Present the Honorable Judges

The Administrators	)	Trover to recover
of Dragging Canoe	)	property. That is to say
decd	)	a negro man Simon
	)	a negro woman Pheby
vs	)	& her children horse,
	)	cattle, hoggs & one
Peggy Pathkiller	)	sett of Black Smith
		tools

The Court gives to the Administrators the negro man Simon four head of grown cows and one set of Blacksmiths tools or two hundred & seventy dollars and costs of suit. John Ridge ___

Witnesses

Chuwalooku	10 days	7.5	$7.50
James Hughs	10 days	75-	7.50
Salley Duck	6 d	75	$4.50
Mrs. Fish	15d	.75-	11.25
Mrs. Head Thrower	16d		10.50
Young Duck	6		4.50
John Thompson	31		23.25
William Thompson	20 d		15.00
Money Cryer	3		2.25

John Ratliff	8	6.00

Hard Nine Months
___ Elijah Hicks

Execution filed 14th August 1829. Delivered to Daniel Griffin one of the Administrators of Dragging Canoe, Decd

RETURNED SATISFIED

Court adjourned to Wednesday morning 10 O'Clock

Wednesday November 5th

Court met according to adjournment
Present the Honorable Judges

Necotiah came in open Court and made Satisfactory proofs that the judgment entered upon him on the 29th Oct. 1827 where James Foreman was Plaintiff was obtained contrary to the intention & meaning of the customs & usages of the Courts of this Nation. It is ordered the Defendant Necotiah do have a new hearing in the case James Foreman vs. Necotiah.

James Foreman	)	Debt on a note of hand
	)	The Court finds for the
vs	)	Defendant
	)	
Necotiah	)	

Ordered that any property that has been collected on a Judgment obtained 29th October 1827 in the case where James Foreman is Plaintiff & Necotiah Defendant be restored to the defendant Necotiah.

<u>Wednesday 5th Nov. 1828</u>

David Vann ______	)	Debt on account
of Peggy Morgan	)	

	)	The Court finds for the
vs	)	Defendant
	)	
Jacob West	)	

Witnesses	Major Ridge	4 days	$3.00
	___Ridge	4 days	3.00
	James Martin	1 day	.75

Court adjourned to thursday morning 10 O'Clock

Thursday 6th Nov. 1828

The Court according to adjournment. Present A. Ross J. Huss and W.S. Adair

Thomas Petit &	)	On a plea of debt arising
David Vann	)	from ___partnership in trade
	)	appertaining to $4271.00
vs	)	
	)	
John Downing	)	
Executor of George	)	The Court finds for the
Downing Dec.	)	Defendant

Witnesses Attendance

Mary Alberty	5 days at Hickory Log	$3.75
at New Echota	7 days	5.25
Salley Allberty	7 "	5.25
Stephen Whelmire	15"	11.25
Thomas Saunders	15	11.25
Wind	15	11.25
James Doherty	15	11.25
Molly Downing	15	11.25
		$70.50

Charles R. Hicks	)	Debt on a let.
by his agents	)	

	)	The Court finds for the Plaintiff a bill of \$471.83½
vs	)	
	)	
John Walker	)	

Court is adjourned to Friday morning 10 O'Oclock

Friday Nov. 7th

Court met according to adjournment Present Andrew Ross, John Huss & W.S. Adair Judges

Court is adjourned to Saturday morning 10 O'Clock

Saturday 8th Nov.

Court met according to adjournment Present Andrew Ross, John Huss & Walter S. Adair

Court is adjourned to Monday morning 10 O'Clock

Monday Nov. 10th

Court met according to adjournment. Present their Honors Andrew Ross, John Huss Walter S. Adair

Joseph Vann	)	Trover to recover a certain property
	)	
vs	)	
	)	The Court decides in favor of the defendants.
David McNair	)	
and Delica McNair	)	

Witnesses carried forward.

Monday Nov. 10

Witnesses attendence

James B. Chisholsm	29 days	-21.75
Clement Vann	34"	25.50
William Burgess	19"	14.25
John Miller	15"	11.25
Major Ridge	7"	5.25
Thomas Pettit	4"	3.00
Big Half Breed	3	2.25
Walking Stick	4	3.00
Chulion	7	5.25
James Foster	10	7.50
James Brown	8	6.00

I do hereby acknowledge myself as security to the judgment against Jos. Vann for nine ____ orders the provisions of this law paper 12 Nov. 1828

13 Nov. 1828 W.S. Goodes

Execution filed delivered 30th Sept. 1829.
Returned satisfied 13th Oct. 1829

John Fields	)	Debt for the price of a horse.
	)	
vs	)	The Court finds a bill of $50. to
	)	be paid in property at valuation
Oowauteyahee	)	

Witnesses

Major Ridge	11 day	7.75
Old Fields	6 days	4.50

Delivered to Sml Adair
Execution issued Nov. 18th 1828

Court is adjourned to Tuesday morning 10 O'Clock

Tuesday morning Nov. 11th

Court met according to adjournment

Present their honors Andrew Ross John Huss Walter S. Adair

Michael Halfacre	)	Damages to recover for an
	)	unlawful seizure of goods
vs	)	
	)	The Court finds for the
Archey Foreman	)	Defendants

Witnesses

Thomas Wilson	8 day	$6.00

Court is adjourned to Wednesday morning 10 O'Clock

Wednesday Nov. 12th

Court met according to adjournment
Present their honors Walter S. Adair

Edward Adair	)	Trover to recover certain negroes
	)	
vs	)	
	)	The Court finds for the
Ambrose Hannage	)	Defendant

Witnesses All

Samuel _eauty	16ds	$12.00
John Wright	10ds	7.50
Nancy Talley	11————————	8.25
James Brown	7——————	5.25
Thomas Pettit	12	9.00
William Hicks	6	4.50
Nancy Hicks	15	11.25
Doctor Murray	7	5.25
William Hicks		

Staid ___ monthly 13th Nov. 1828 W.S. Adair, Security

Executions issued, delivered to Jos. M. Lynch Marshal May 15th 1829

Nancy Dougherty	)	Damage assault and battery
	)	
vs	)	
	)	The Court gives to the Plaintiff
Thomas Monroe	)	Six dollars

Execution issued Nov. 19th 1828
Satisfied and returned by Joseph M. Lynch ML 15th May 1829

Court adjourned until Thursday morning 10 O'Clock

<u>Thursday November 13th</u>

Court met according to adjournment. Present their Honors Andrew Ross John Huss and Walter S. Adair

Dunham Orr	)	Action for debt
	)	
vs	)	
	)	The Court finds a bill for the
Chickasarotehee	)	Plaintiff for $8.00

Witnesses
John Love 8 days $6.00

Archey Foreman	)	Charged for a violation of the law
for	)	
Cherokee Nation	)	
	)	
vs	)	
	)	Court finds for the deft.
William Mjeunkize	)	

Witnesses
Major Martin 12 days 75——$9.00

Robert Smith	)	To recover a stolen mare
by his agt David Ross	)	

	)	
vs	)	
	)	The Court finds for the plaintiff
David England	)	$60.00

Execution issued Nov. 20th 1828

James Turk	)	Debt on judgment from McMinn
	)	County Tennessee
vs	)	
	)	The Court finds for the
c & JW Agnew	)	Defendant.

Thursday Nov. 13th

Andrew M. Vann	)	Debt on acts.
agt. For Major Henderson	)	
	)	
vs	)	
	)	The Court Confirms the
Samuel Talley	)	judgment of the District Court
	)	of $74.75

Execution issued Nov. 18th 1828

Joseph Goodsy	)	Debt on note
for the use of Haslerig	)	
& Rawlins	)	
	)	
vs	)	
	)	The Court finds for the Plaintiffs
Hugh Price	)	seventy four dollars & interest
	)	from 7th Sept. 1827 to Nov. 13th
	)	1828

I do hereby acknowledge myself as security for Hugh Price for six monthly _ay on this judgment obtained in favor of J. Goody for the use of Haselrig & Rawlins. R. Taylor

Execution issued June 10th 1829

John Walker	)	Debt on acct
	)	
vs	)	
	)	Debarred by the Constitution Act.
John Jourdan, Jr	)	

The adjourned until the second Monday in October next.

W.S. Adair
Andrew Ross
In Cherokee (John Huss??)

Court adjourned to the Second Monday of October 1829—

<u>October Term 1829 of the Supreme Ct.</u>

<u>Monday 12th</u>

The Court met according to adjournment

Present Walter S. Adair Andrew Ross John Huss Judges

Court is adjourned to Tuesday 10 O'Clock

<u>Tuesday 13th</u>

The Court met according to adjournment

Present Walter S. Adair Andrew Ross Jno Huss Judges

Court is adjourned to Wednesday 10 O'Clock

Wednesday 14th

The Court met according to adjournment

Present The Hon Judges

<u>October Term 1829 of the Supreme Ct.</u>

Elizabeth Pettit	)	Debt on contract
	)	
vs	)	
	)	
James Pettit	)	

The Court finds for the Plaintiff sixty four dollars to be paid in young cattle <u>at valuation</u>.

Execution issued 20th October 1829

Court is adjourned to Thursday 10 O'Clock.

<u>Thursday 15th</u>

The Court met according to adjournment

Court is adjourned to Friday 10 O'Clock

Court met according to adjournment
Present the Hon Judges

<u>Friday 16th October</u>

Court adjourned Saturday 10 O'Clock

Saturday 17th

Court met according to adjournment

Present the Hon Judges

Wyckoff Pickens ___	)	Debt on note
	)	
vs	)	
	)	
Andrew Ross &	)	Judgment in favor of the Plaintiff
Elizabeth Pack	)	for twenty one hundred seventy
	)	three dollars $ sixty nine cents &
	)	costs of suit.

Execution issued delivered to Jos. M. Lynch No Marshal Nov 1829

Jesse Watkins	)	Recover damages for a certain
	)	horse
vs	)	
	)	The court find for the Plaintiff
David Thompson	)	fifty dollars and cost of suit to be
	)	discharged in good property at
	)	valuation 17th October 1829

Cost of appeal paid 21st Oct 1829 execution issued

Betsey Walker	)	Replevy of property on
	)	attachment Say three negroes
vs	)	
	)	**The court finds for the Plaintiff**
David Vann	)	

Saturday Oct 17th

Betey Walker	)	Replevy for attent
	)	
vs	)	
	)	The Court find for the Plaintiff.
David Vann	)	

Costs Witnesses

Pd to Mrs. Walker	Jesse Bushyhead	$6.75
Pd to J. Foreman	Nancy Springstove	7.50
		$14.25

Court adjourned to Monday morning 10 O'Clock

Monday 19th

Court met according to adjournment.
Present W.S. Adair Andrew Ross John Huss Judges

Monday 19th

Court adjourned to Tuesday 9 O'Clock

Tuesday 20th

Court met according to adjournment

David Vann, Agt	)	Recover $100 Bill
for S. T. Mays	)	
	)	
vs	)	
	)	The Court find for the Deft.
S. Spaniard	)	

John Hill	)	Debt on act
	)	
vs	)	
	)	The Court finds for the plaintiff
Templin W. Ross	)	sixteen dollars and six and a
	)	fourth cents.

Execution issued 26 October 1829

Court adjourned to Wednesday 10 O'Clock

Wednesday 21st

Court met according to adjournment
Present the Hon Judges

Wednesday 21st October

Horace Broom	)	Recover for a stolen horse
	)	
vs	)	
	)	The Court acquit the defts 21st
Nancy & Sally Miller	)	Oct.

S Ballard	)	Debt on note
	)	
vs	)	
	)	The court find for the defendend
Jno Helderbrand	)	
Cherokee Nation	)	On the charge of
	)	**murder The Court concur with**
vs	)	**the decition of**
	)	The sentence having been passed
	)	in the Circuit Court,
	)	this Court decide that they have
	)	no power **to take it up.**
Noo. Cha. Wee.	)	of suspending the sentence of
	)	said Circuit Court 19th October.

Court adjourned to Thursday morning 10 O'Clock

Thursday 22nd October

Court met according to adjournment
Present the hon Judges

Cherokee Nation	)	Hiring a citizen of the U.S.
	)	
vs	)	
	)	The Court fine the Deft ten
George Harlan	)	dollars

Execution returned satisfied 4 October 1830

The Court adjourned to Friday morning 10 O'Clock

Friday 23rd

Court met according to adjournment.

Robt Brown	)	Recover damages on note traded
	)	by the deft
vs	)	
	)	Judgment in favor of the Deft.
Rider Fields	)	

Court adjourned to Saturday morning 10 O'Clock

Saturday 24th

The Court met according to adjournment. Present their honours Andrew Ross, John Huss & W.S. Adair Judges of the Supreme Court

Court adjourned to Monday morning 10 O'Clock

<u>Monday 26th</u>

The Court met according to adjournment—Present their honours Andrew Ross, John Huss and Walter S. Adair—Judges

<u>Monday 26th October</u>

A. McCoy vs George Hicks	)))))	Walter S. Adair was objected to by the Deft.
A. McCoy vs George Hicks	)))))	Recover of ferry landing and damages The Court find for the Deft

Execution issued
Witnesses attendance Major Ridge—.75
William Hicks—.75

Court adjourned to Tuesday morning 10 O'Clock

<u>Tuesday 27th</u>

The Court met according to adjournment. Present the honourable Judges Andrew Ross, John Huss, Walter S. Adair.

The case A Harnage **being called and W.S. Adair being** vs. A. McCoy being called W.S. Adair being objected by the plaintiff

<u>October Term 1829</u>

Court adjourned to to Wednesday morning 10 O'Clock

<u>The Wensday 28th</u>

The Court met according to adjournment. Present the hon. Judges of the Supreme Court—

Ambrose Harnage vs	)))	Debt on a note

	)	The Court find for the Defendant
Alex McCoy	)	

Execution Issued
Witnesses Attendance Jos. P. Chisholm—56 days——42.00
Chah wah ee gah—56 days——42.00

Wensday 28th

Elizabeth Sutton	)	Trover to recover for a plantation
	)	
vs	)	
	)	
Thos Berry	)	The Court find for the Deft
Rick Edmonson	)	

An Order given to the National Office to take possession of the plantation

John McGowen	)	Debt on note
	)	
vs	)	
	)	Discontinued on the grounds
The heirs of Jno. Lowrey,	)	that the note being brought
Decd	)	into Court

Jno. Martin	)	Debt on Judgment
	)	
vs	)	
	)	The Court give judgment in favor
Edward Adair	)	of the plaintiff for thirty four
	)	dollars & ten cents. Interest
	)	twenty two dollars, forty eight
	)	cents & dollars & fifty cents for
	)	costs in a former judgment
	)	making the whole sixty seven
	)	dollars & eight cents $67.08

October Term 1829

Nelly	)	Recover property
	)	
vs	)	
	)	**The Court find for the defendant.**
Catherine Smith	)	Discontinued for non-attendance.
	)	
	)	

Jno Baldridge	)	Recover for a plantation
	)	
vs	)	
	)	Dismissed by default.
Jesse Raper	)	

Court adjourned until Thursday 10 O'Clock

Friday 29th Thursday

The Court med according to adjournment Present their honors Andrew Ross, John Huss and Walter S. Adair, Judges.

Friday Thursday 29th

Hetty Vickry	)	Trover to recover property
	)	
vs	)	
	)	The Court decide in favor of the
	)	defendant as debarred by the
	)	Darcus Hummingbird
	)	limitation act

Eliza Eliott	)	Slander
	)	
vs	)	
	)	The Court find for the defendant
Eliza Post	)	

Execution issued November 17th 1829
Witnesses attendance——Mrs. Ruthy Phillips 6 days—$4.50

William Nave	)	Debt on account
	)	
vs	)	
	)	The Court give judgment for
Spanish Peter	)	plaintiff five dollars.

Execution issued November 1829

October Term 1829

Court adjourned to Friday morning at 10 O'Clock

Friday 30th

The Court met according to adjournment. Present the honorable Judges.

William Richardson	)	Debt on account
	)	
vs	)	
	)	Judgment in favor of the Plaintiff
	)	one hundred and seventy four—
Ambrose Harnage	)	dollars thirty seven and a half
	)	cents

I do hereby acknowledge myself security to the to stay the above judgment attained against Abrose Harnage in favor of William Richardson agreeable to law.

John Martin

Cherokee Nation	)	Gaming at cards
	)	
vs	)	
	)	Judgment against the defendant
Thomas J. Pack	)	fifty dollars.

Friday 30th

Choo, wa, loogee	)	Recover damages for a fraud in
	)	**exchange of** a horse.
vs	)	
	)	The Court find for the Defendant
E. Edwards	)	
	)	

John Brown	)	Assault and battery
	)	
vs	)	
	)	The case having been tried in a
Spanish Peter	)	circuit Court this Court
	)	have decided that they have **has**
	)	no power to take it up.

Thos. J. Davis	)	Debt on note
for the use of Geo. Gunter	)	
	)	
vs	)	
	)	Judgment by default against the
J. Maulkey	)	Defendant one hundred
	)	and thirty dollars with interest
	)	from the first of Nov. 1827.

Execution issued 6th Nov. 1829

October Term 1829

Treasury of the Nation	)	Debt on note
	)	
vs	)	
	)	
Elijah Hicks	)	The Court find give a verdict
Geo M. Lavender	)	against the Defts
& Jas Daniel	)	ninety dollars with interest from
	)	the 19th of Nov. 1827

Staid nine months Leonard Hicks security
Execution issued 4th October 1830

Court adjourned to Saturday morning 10 O'Clock.

<u>Saturday 31st</u>

The Court met according to adjournment. Present the Honorable Judges Andrew Ross, John Huss Walter S. Adair, Judges

Thomas B. Adair	)	Recover damage for moving a
	)	house
vs	)	
	)	The Court concur with the
Alex Feather	)	Nation C.C. Hightower Dist.
	)	for twelve dollars and fifty cents

Saturday 31st October 1829

Andrew M. Vann	)	Debt on note
	)	
vs	)	
	)	The Court give a judgment in
Saml Adair, Jr.	)	favor of the ptff for
	)	two cows and calves and sixteeen
		hundred # of beef.

Jesse Raper	)	Trover for a plantation
	)	
vs	)	
	)	Judgment in favor of the
Tao. Nah. Na. Lah	)	defendant

Lanee Dick	)	The Court confirm with the
	)	District Court in favor of
vs	)	the Plaintiff
	)	
Polly Barnett	)	

Court adjourned to the Second Monday of October 1830. A Ross John Huss W.S. Adair

<u>October Term 1830</u>

George Baldridge came in and had the following affidavits recorded

Cherokee Nation)
Chattogee District)

Sept. 27th 1830

Personally came before me in open Court, Walter Adair, Circuit Judge, James Spencer & after being during sworn according to law, deposeth and saith, that he was present when Luther Morgan gave to George Baldridge a bill of sale of a certain negroe Woman named Silver and knew of his being in possession of said negroe and bill of sale. Sworn to and subscribed the day and date above written.

Walter Adair James X Spencer
Judge C.C. His Mark

Cherokee Nation)
Cha Loo Ga Dist)

Sept. 27th 1830

Personally came before me in open Court, Walter Adair, Circuit Judge, Charles Dry Head and after being duly sworn deposeth that he acted as interpreter between George Baldridge and—when the said Baldridge bought a certain negroe girl named Hannah and saw the said Give to the said Baldridge a bill of sale of said negroe girl. Sworn to and subscribed the day and date above written

Walter Adair Charles Dry X Fore Head
Judge C.C. His Mark

Cherokee Nation)
Cha Loo Ga Dist)

Sept. 27th 1830

Personally came before me in open Court Walter Adair, Circuit Judge, George Baldridge and after being duly sworn according to law deposeth that on the night of 7th of ___ last he was robed of certain property trunk DC together with two bills of sale of two negroes one a girl Silver by name aged as near can be recollected about twenty years the other a girl Hannah by name age also not recollected but about nine years old, and the above bill of sale of Silver was made to him by Luther Morgan when living in Huntsville, and the other bill of sale of Hannah was made to him by Latte & Failds. Sworn to and subscribed the and date above written

Walter Adair	Geo X Baldridge
Judge J.C.C.	His Mark

<u>October Term 1830</u>

Saturday 16th

On account of the Marshal being not here the Court did not meet until today. Present the honorable Judges of the Supreme Court Walter S. Adair, Andrew Ross, Jno Huss and S Watie Clerk.

John Harrison	)	On a note of hand for $75.00
for the use of Jno Graves	)	
	)	
vs	)	
	)	The Court find for the defendant
The heirs of Jno Lowney	)	
decd	)	

The Court adjourned until Monday morning at 10 O'Clock

<u>Monday 18th</u>

The Court met according to adjournment. Present Walter S. Adair Andrew Ross John Huss, Judges

October Term 1830

Widow Cornblade	)	Recover for a horse
	)	
vs	)	
	)	The Court find for the plaintiff
James Fields	)	the horse contended for or fifty
	)	dollars in trade at valuation

The Court adjourned until to morrow morning at ten O'Clock

Tuesday 19th

The Court met according to adjournment. Present hon. Judges Walter S. Adair Andrew Ross and Jno Huss.

The Court adjourned to tomorrow morning at ten o'clock.

Wednesday 20th

The Court met according to adjournment Present the hon. Judges W. S. Adair Andrew Ross and John Huss.

October Term 1830

Crying Snake	)	Trippes to try the right of a
	)	certain field at Pathkiller's ferry
vs	)	on the west side of the river.
	)	The Court find for the plaintiff,
Robert Brown	)	Crying Snake, the field in dispute

Witnesses Attendance

M. McIntosh	14 days—$10.50
John Ratliff	17 days—12.75
Chnoky	16 "——12.00

James Lasley	15 "——11.25
Yeakey	3 "——2.25
Lakey	2 "——1.50
Kenah	6 "——4.50
Kah,Lo,Ne, Sky	3 "——2.25

John Ridge	)	To try the right a certain
	)	improvement and houses
vs	)	adjoining the plantation of Jack
	)	Quahquh decd lying
	)	east and west of on the road to
	)	Oongrillogee
Shade Qua,quah	)	The Court find find for the
and others	)	Plaintiff the field and houses
	)	in dispute

October Term 1830

Tom Boot	)	Trove to recover a cow
	)	
vs	)	
	)	The Court find for the defendant
Dav. McNair	)	

The Court adjourned to tomorrow morning at ten o'clock

<u>Thursday 21st</u>

The Court met according to adjournment
Present as yesterday W.S. Adair Andrew Ross and Jno Huss, Judges

John McCarver	)	**Debt on note**
M. Gore by their agent	)	
McConnell	)	
	)	
vs	)	
	)	**The Court find for the Plaintiff**
John Martin	)	**nineteen dollars forty four**
	)	**cents and a half**

This was an action

John McCarver &	)	This was an action brought on a
Maurice Gore by their	)	note of hand executed
agent	)	about the first day of January,
Saml McConnell	)	1830 and due the first of March
	)	following the sum of three
	)	hundred and fifty dollars by
	)	John Martin to the above
	)	McCarver and Gore.
vs	)	
	)	
John Martin	)	

And it appearing to the satisfaction of the Court that the said note was given in part of the consideration of three negroes and it also appearing that a negroe woman one of the three was unsound at the time and that said negroe with said complaint also that the said plaitiffs purchased her as unsound property and willfully practiced a fraud by vending the same. It is adjuged by the Court, that the plaintiff recover of the defendant only nineteen dollars and forty four and a half cents for his debt and cost of suit in his behalf expended.

October Term 1830

Widow Root	)	Debt for a horse
	)	
vs	)	
	)	The Court find for the Defendant

The Katcher)

The Court adjourned to tomorrow morning at ten o'clock

Friday 22nd

Court met according to adjournment. Present the hon. Judges W.S. Adair, Andrew Ross and John Huss

Betsey Walker	)	Recover damages for unlawfully
	)	detaining negroes
vs	)	
	)	The Court find for the Defendant
David Vann	)	

Court adjourned to Saturday morning at ten o'clock

October Term 1830

Saturday 23rd

Court met according to adjournment. Present their honors, Walter S. Adair, Andrew Ross & John Huss, Judges

George Harlin	)	Debt on a/c
by his agent Eli Harlin	)	
	)	
vs	)	
	)	The Court find for the Plaintiff
Michael Huffacre	)	four hundred and twenty
	)	six dollars and thirty one and a
	)	fourth cents.

Cost
Witnesses Attendance

Edward Adair	19 days	$14.25
Archey Foreman	17 days	12.75

Execution issued Jan 8th, 1831

William Post	)	Trespass to recover a field
	)	
vs	)	
	)	The Court decide that the corner
	)	starting from a pine tree
Samuel Mays	)	on the hill and running a straight
	)	**line** direction to the

mouth of the hollow, near the corner of Post's field dividing between the parties shall be the true line, and that the National Marshal as soon as convenient proceed to the place notifying the parties & mark the line.

<u>October Term 1830</u>

M. Hildebrand	)	This case was brought up from
	)	the Circuit Court on a point of
	)	law and it is decided that the case
vs	)	be taken up in
	)	the Circuit Court for trial.
James Pettit	)	

Charles Thornton	)	Debt on note
	)	
vs	)	
	)	The Court give Judgment in favor
Walter Adair	)	of the Plaintiff for
	)	eighty five dollars and seventy
	)	five cents with lawful interest
	)	from the fifteenth of Dec. 1829.

I do hereby acknowledge myself as security to stay the above judgment for six months according to law.

Samuel Mays

Robt. Paris	)	<u>Case on a Bond</u>

	)	
vs	)	
	)	
John Gillen and	)	The Court find for the Plaintiff
Giles McAnulty	)	seventy five dollars each.

Court adjourned until Monday morning ten o'clock.

October Term 1830

Saturday 25th

The Court met according to adjournment. Present Walter S. Adair Andrew Ross Jno Huss Judges

Jesse Halfbreed	)	Debt on notes and a/c
	)	
vs	)	
	)	The Court find for the Plaintiff
Samual Copeland	)	eleven dollars and seventy five
	)	cent and the wagon bed to be
	)	valued by men that may be
	)	chosen by the parties and the
	)	value thereof to be placed to the
	)	credit of said judgment.

Appeal Cost—— $.75 paid to Martin

Court adjourned to Tuesday morning at ten o'clock 26th

Tuesday 26th

Court met according to adjournment. Present their Hon Judges W.S. Adair Andrew Ross and John Huss

October Term 1830

Chelsey	)	Recover for a horse
	)	
vs	)	
	)	The Court find for the Defendant
Wah, Ta, Ne, Tah	)	

Witnesses Attendance

Cah, Ne, Doo,	One Day	.75
Sarah	1 day	.75
Wahtey	1 day	.75

Saran and Henry	)	Debt on due bill
Pierce	)	
	)	
vs	)	
	)	Judgment in favor of the Plaintiff
James P. Chisholm	)	twenty four dollars

It is ordered that David Vann be notified by the Clerk to be and appear personally on the first day of the term of the Supreme Court at New Echota to be holder for the Cherokee Nation. 1831, to show cause if any, why there should not be a new trial granted in the case Elizabeth Walker vs **David Vann** agent for the children for the children of Peggy Morgan vs. David Vann for unlawfully detaining certain negroes. October 26th 1830

Quaty Adair	)	Debt on note
	)	
vs	)	
	)	The Court find for the Plaintiff
George Caudy	)	eight dollars

NOTE **There are no entries for 1831*****

Supreme Court of the Cherokee Nation

October Term 1832

Wednesday October 17th

Present their Hons. John Huss & Walter S. Adair

Court adjourned to Thursday morning at 10 o'clock

Thursday 18th

The Court met according to adjournment. Present as yesterday

Sally Hawkins	)	Appeal from the bench
	)	
vs	)	
	)	The Court decide that the case be
	)	remanded to the court below
Betsey Welch	)	for trial.

The Court adjourned to Friday morning 10 o'clock.

Friday 19th October

The Court met according to adjournment. Present the Hon. Judges John Huss & Walter S. Adair

Their being no business ready for trial, the Court adjourned until tomorrow 10 o'clock.

October Term 1832

Saturday 20th Oct.

The Court met according to adjournment. Present as yesterday.

The Court adjourned until Monday 9 o'clock

Monday 22nd Oct.

Court met according to adjournment. Present as on Saturday.

The Flint	)	Trover to recover for a horse
	)	
vs	)	
	)	The Court find for the Deft
Richard Walker	)	

Court adjourned until tomorrow 9 o'clock

Tuesday 23rd

Court met according to adjournment. Present as on yesterday.

James Foreman	)	Debt on note for cattle
	)	
vs	)	
	)	
J_sae Bushyhead &	)	Judgement for sixteen dollars and
Jesse Bushyhead	)	seventy five cents

October Term 1832

Cooliah	)	To recover for a _____.
	)	
vs	)	
	)	The Court find for the Deft.
James Foreman	)	

Court adjourned until tomorrow nine o'clock

Wednesday 24nd

Court met according to adjournment. Present as yesterday.

Robert Vann	)	Appeal from the bench of
	)	Chick.ee
vs	)	
	)	Remanded back for trial.

Geo. Benge	)	
Sally Lowry	)	Tro. to recover 7 head of cattle
	)	
vs	)	
	)	We the Court for for Ptff 7 head
Archy Foreman	)	cattle Cost forty dollars $40.00

Execution issued on 1 day Nov. 1832

October Term 1832

Court adjourned until tomorrow nine o'clock

Thursday 25

Court met according to adjournment. Present as on yesterday.

Tan. Chu. Lah. Nah	)	Trover to recover a certain black
	)	horse
vs	)	
	)	The Court find for the Deft
Ah. Nah. Tu. Kee	)	

The Court having no other business before them they have adjourned until the second Monday in October next.

Court adjourned until tomorrow nine o'clock

Friday 26th

Court met according to adjournment. Present John Huss Geo. Waters and Wm Caudy the two latter having been selected by the Committee to sit in the place of Lewis Ross and W.S. Adair

A. McCoy	)	Debt on an order
	)	
vs	)	

	)	The Court find for the Plaintiff
David Minor	)	thirty dollars

Execution issued on November 1832.

The Court having no other business before them they have adjourned until the second Monday Oct. next.

CHEROKEE NATION)
NORTH CAROLINA)

This will testify that we the undersigned Cherokee of the State of North Carolina were residents of the Nation at the time that a white man and an Indian trader who had a Cherokee woman for his wife but who by his usage of her by beating and other wise mistreating of her when of pregnancy died the Clan or Tribe to whom she belonged determined to kill the said white man by name of Tom Dent who to appease them and satisfy said Tribe or Clan went off to Augusta in Georgia and did then purchase a female slave name of Molly and brought female unto the Cherokee Nation and did offer her to the Clans remunerations for the wrongs he had done, a Town Council & Talk was then had at Chata Old Town on Tennessee River and the said female was then and and there received by D Clan and by the authorities agreeable to the Indian Law and usage in the place of the murdered wife of the said Tom Dent and has by her self and descendants been since recognized by said Nation or Clan as a Cherokee this Said Molly and her descendants now whose the only descendants of said Molly has been and are claimed to be the property of one Massey Hightower who has come unto the said Nation and let up claim by Bill of Sale for Said Tom Dent to D. Hightower's father, who was also an Indian trader and who lived many years near the descendants of said and ___ ____ for set up any claim to ths said descendants that the present Petitioner claims to to Alias Isaac Tucker and his mother Chickawa was ___ off in these by force mentioned natives as we has ever be conscious. The Court and authorities of the Cherokee Nation as also we the sub ___ members of the same Clan ask and require of our Council and head men for assistance and for council to resist this oppressive and illegal wrong attempt to be practiced on our Brothers and Sisters by the Hightower in _____ in to slavery two of whom have ever been and considered native Cherokees in full that the attempt is one of cruel grievance to us and ask of you Honorable bodies redress in the protection and defer of the two afore mentioned members of our Clan and your Petitioners will ever prove.

&& The Doctor	)	The Old The Gh his mark
Chis nes Tustee Adasi his mark	)	Bucks Horn his mark
Isaac Tucker	)	Chicked Indian Man
Chickawa ne Molly her mark	)	
Charles Buffington	)	

This day appeared before me Daniel McCoy one of the Judges of the Supreme Court of the Cherokee Nation the Big Half Breed Jno Watts the Tiger and the White Path who being duly sworn and sayeth that to the best of their knowledge and belief that the mother of Edward & Isaac Tucker Molly was surrendered and delivered up when a girl some time previous to the Revolutionary War by a white man named Saml Bend to the authorities of the Cherokee Nation for certain important considerations and that said Molly was then manifested & adopted into the Clan composing the Deer family agreeably to the then existing usages & customs of said Nation. & Since that time she has continued in the Nation & enjoyed the liberty of freedom & that her two sons Edward & Isaac Tucker were born at the beloved Town called Echota on the Tennessee River & has ever been free & resided in the Nation.

Sworn to & Subscribed before me at Red Clay this 18th Oct. 1833.

Daniel McCoy	Signed Big Half Breed his + mark
J. S. Court	White Path his + Mark
	Jno Watts his + Mark
	Tiger his + Mark

I certify that the above to be a correct copy of the original delivered to the said Isaac Tucker

18th October 1833	)	Charles Vann
	)	Clerk Supreme Court

<u>October Term 1833</u>

Saturday 19th

The Court met according to adjournment. Present Danl McCoy, John Huss & W.S. Adair, Judges

The Court appointed Charles H. Vann Clerk—

Betsy Walker, agent	)	Sci. Fa. For a new Trial
for Peggy Morgan Children	)	
	)	
vs	)	
	)	The Court refused to grant the
David Vann	)	Trial

The Court adjourned till Monday 10 O'clock

Monday 21st October

The Court met according to adjournment. Present W.S. Adair, John Huss Daniel McCoy Judges

<u>October 21st 1833—</u>

Cathy McDaniel for and	)	Trespass to recover damages
in the behalf of her son	)	$15.00
John B. McDaniel	)	
	)	
vs	)	
	)	Court find for Defendant 21
Jesse Raper	)	October 1833

Tuesday 22nd

Court met according to adjournment—Present as on yesterday

October 22nd

Delila McLane	)	Trespass to recover improvements
	)	
vs	)	

	)	The Court find for the Defendant
Joseph Spears	)	

Michael Watkins	)	Johnson Foreman & Judgment in
	)	favor of the Plaintiff
vs	)	for ninety six dollars & fifty cents
	)	
John Butler	)	

M. Watkins due 16th June 1833
W. Let for appeal $5.73
Execution issued 25th October

<u>October Term 1833</u>

Smokies	)	Debt on note
	)	
vs	)	$37
	)	1.48 $38.48
Archd Foreman	)	Judgment for Ptff
& Jos. Spears	)	22nd Oct 1833

Thos. Mannon	)	Debt on acct
	)	$10.00
vs	)	
	)	Judgment for Ptff ten dollars &
Young Wolf	)	cost 22nd Oct

Thos C Wrae	)	Debt on note
	)	$20 $22.40
vs	)	<u>2.40</u>
	)	Judgment for Ptff for twenty
Arch. d Foreman	)	dollars due 19th July 1833 &
	)	cost 22nd Oct

Court adjourned until tomorrow morning ten O'clock

Wednesday Oct 23rd

Court convened according to adjournment
Present as on yesterday

<u>October 23rd</u>

T. W. Ross	)	Debt on note
	)	Judgment for Ptf for five dollars
vs	)	& fifty cents with interest from
	)	27th August 1820
Sleeping Rabit	)	23rd Oct. 1833

George Still	)	Debt on acct.
	)	\$50.00
vs	)	\$25
	)	
Peggy	)	Judgment for Plaintiff for fifty
	)	five dollars and costs

Salley Murphy	)	Debt on account
	)	
vs	)	
	)	
Robt. Fields	)	Judgment for Defendant 24th
	)	October

John Walker, Sr.	)	Debt
	)	
vs	)	
	)	Judgment for Defendant
Samuel Larkins	)	Oct 24

Cherokee Nation
In the Charter Limits of Alabor
February 25th 1833

To all whom it may concern. Know ye by these presents that I Richard Ratliff being now advanced in years and not knowing how soon the great God whom I adore as my maker may call me out of this probationary state of existence on earth and moreover being sound by the blessings of providence in mind has in consideration of this great love my daughter Jinney the wife of Daniel Griffin for has for me and in consideration of the equal affection that I entertain for her have short pro___ to make this deed of gift to the said Jinney & and titles there of certain negroes to wit Fanny and her children Haner Joe and Lily and all their increase and Patty and her two children named Beckey and Peter and negroe woman named Mary which title and all right of mine appertaining I have by transfer and make over and invest to my daughter from this day in order that she may hold keep and retain the said negroes and their increase free from all claims and I do moreover obligate myself to defend the same to her the said Jinney her heirs and assigns from my Self my heirs and assigns and from all persons whosoever. Done at the place and date above written in the presence of the under signed as witness my hand and seal.

Richard Ratliff (seal)

Witness Edward Gray

I do certify the above to be a true copy of the original.

24th Oct. 1833	)	Charles H. Vann
	)	Clerk Supreme Court
	)	Ch. Nat.

David Thompson	)	Debt
	)	
vs	)	
	)	Court find for Defendant
David Ross	)	24th Oct. 1833

Court adjourned to tomorrow morning 10 O'clock

Friday 25th Oct

Court convened according to adjournment present as on yesterday

David Leonatoyee	)	Debt on note
	)	
vs	)	
	)	Court find for Plaintiff

Che Coo. Ece	)	Fifty dollars in trade
	)	25 Oct, 1833

Execution issued 30th Oct. 1833

Nancy Hawkins	)	On a debt
	)	
vs	)	
	)	Court find for Plaintiff two
Wm Loudermilk	)	hundred & thirty dollars
	)	25th Oct, 1833

Execution issued 31st Oct. 1833

Know all men by these presents that I Mary Stedman of the District of Chockaman Goo and Cherokee Nation have this day for goods and sold to Joseph Vann of the District of Coosawatie and Nation aforesaid the following described property being one negroe woman ____ by the name of Jinny about fifty years old also her husband named Harry about the same age and her children Sally thirty four years old, Charlot twenty eight years old George, twenty six Rosanna twenty one, Isaac eighteen Bob sixteen Harry fourteen Caty eleven and Elllack eight years old and her the said Jinney's grandchildren Ruben nine Washington six, Salley three and Ereline one year old also ten head of cattle one ___ mare and two colts one bay horse and poney and one waggon for consideration of the sum of four thousand and twenty dollars to me in hand for the receipt whereof is hereby acknowledged Witness my hand and Seal this tenth day of August 1829.

Mary Stedman (seal)

Test

George M. Lavender	)
John Bell	)

Cherokee Nation

Personally came George M. Lavender before me and made oath in due form deposeth and saith that he saw Mary Stedman seal and deliver the within bill of sale for the use therein set forth and that John Bell was a Sub ____ witness with himself to the ___ same Sworn to and subscribed before me this 24 Oct 1833

George M. Lavender

WS Adair Judge SC
I do certify the afore to be a true copy of the original

24th Oct 1833

Charles H. Vann
Clerk Supreme Court Ch Nation

Oct Term 1833
Friday 25—

Arch Acorn	)	Court find for Defendant
	)	
vs	)	
	)	
Moses Hildebrand	)	25th Oct. 1833

Cloud	)	Trover to recover for cattle 4 head
	)	
vs	)	
	)	Court find for Ptf the four head
	)	of cattle or the value of the
Spanish Peter	)	goods _____ this property
	)	25th Oct. 1833

Execution filed 31st Oct 1833

James C. Martin	)	Ord. of ___set
	)	
vs	)	
	)	Court find for Defendant
Jos. Petit	)	25th Oct 1833

Amos Thornton	)	Damages to recover for false
	)	imprisonment
vs	)	

	)	Judgment for defendents
James Foreman and others	)	October 26th 1833

October Term 1833

Richard Anderson	)	Assault and Battery to recover
	)	damages
vs	)	
	)	Court find for Plft five dollars
	)	and cost of suit
Dav Otter Lifter	)	26th Oct. 1833

Execution filed 1st day of Nov. 1833

Court adjourned until Monday morning nine o'clock

Monday 28th Oct.

Court convened according to adjournment.
Present W.S. Adair, John Huss

October Term

Betsey Walker	)	Trespass for improvement
	)	
vs	)	
	)	Court find for the Plaintiff from
Young Wolf	)	her new improvement
	)	October 28th

October Term

Nicholis Smith	)	Trover to recover hogs
	)	
vs	)	
	)	Court find for the Plaintiff
Ooh ___Wah Soto	)	twenty hogs
	)	Oct 28th

The Court adjourned until the 2nd Monday in October next.

October Term 1834

Thursday 23rd October

Court met according to adjournment. Present W.S. Adair, Daniel McCoy & Arch.Fields, Judges

Thursday October 23rd 1834

Sally Timberlake	)	Trover to by the right of a filly &
	)	four head of cattle
vs	)	
	)	This Court find for the Plaintiff
Fadden & Wife Susan	)	the year old filly or the value
	)	thereof in other good property.

The Court adjourns till tomorrow morning 10 o'clock

Friday 24th

Court convened according to adjournment. Present as yesterday

Ta chak Keesee	)	Debt $10.00 forfeit in horse swap
	)	
vs	)	
	)	Court find for Plaintiff ten dollars
Robin Perry	)	24th Oct. 1834
Cost of appeal 00.60¢		

Defined myself to stand R. Perry's property for amount of Judgment against said Perry. Oolayoua his X mark

Court adjourned till tomorrow morning 9 o'clock

Saturday October 25th

Court met according to adjournment. Present as on yesterday

Sokon ah tah hee	)	Debt for horse
	)	
vs	)	
	)	Judgment for Defendant
A. Toh La Hee	)	

To all and singular to whom it may concern, Know ye that for and in consideration of the sum of one hundred and fifty dollars received from Prince a black man slave we do by these presents emancipate and set him free and will defend him against the caim or claims of any other person or persons whatever. In witness where of we have here unto let our hands and seals this 20th day of January 1834.

Witnesses Present		
Lewis Ross	)	Caty Richmond her X mark
John Miller	)	Annoy Richmond his X mark
		Big Drum his X mark

I do certify that the above is a true coppy of the original. Charles Vann S.C. Ch. Na.

25th day of October 1834

Saturday Oct. 25th 1834

Pheasant	)	Trover for 5 head of cattle
	)	
vs	)	
	)	Court find for Pltf. the five head
Tiesley & Brothers	)	of Cattle or the value thereof
	)	in other good property.
	)	25th Oct. 1834

Execution issued 3 Dec. 1834

Court adjourned until Monday morning 9 o'clock

Monday 27th Oct. 1834

Court met according to adjournment. Present W.S. Adair A Field & Daniel McCoy Judges SC

Culstah.yee	Trover 1 cow and six years increase
vs	
George Cherokee	Court find for Defendant 27th Oct. 1834

Court adjourned until tomorrow 9 o'clock

Tuesday 28th

Court met according to adjournment. Present as on yesterday Their Hons SC

Sally Hawkins	Trover to recover a cow & her increase 12 years
vs	
Betsey Welch	The Court find for the Ptf thirty dollars to be discharged in good trade at a fair valuation

Court adjourned until tomorrow nine o'clock

Wednesday 29th

Court met according to adjournment. Present as on yesterday. Their Hons. SC

Wednesday 29-

Cherokee Nation	Charged with the crime of murder

vs)
)
The Broom)

Jurors for the trial
John Butler
Arch Foreman
Con ne que yoh kee
Nee La Kah
Dick Sander
Fishing Hawk
Fox Taylor
John Love
Roman ____
Ao Se Nah Leo
Adrian McCrary
Samuel Foreman
We the Jury find a verdict of not guilty. Saml. Foreman
Foreman

The Court adjourned until tomorrow nine o'clock

Thursday 30

The Honorable Supreme Court met agreeable to adjournment. Present as on yesterday their Hons. SC

Cherokee Nation) Theft hog stealing
)
vs)
)
Choonoolaskee)
Rain Crow)
Sleeping Rabbit)

We the jury find Choonoolaskee guilty of hog stealing & find ten dollars for the hogs so stolen & acquit Rain Crow & S. Rabbit
Saml. Foreman
Fore

Jurors chosen & sworn to try this case, are as follows: Saml Foreman, Charles Timberlake, Ned Five Roller, Black Fox, Keel Ka Los Kee, and Wee Loo Ka—

Court is adjourned until the Second Monday in October next. Court is in accord.

October 1835

Saturday 24th

The Honorable Supreme Court met agreeable to adjournment. Present their Hons. W.S. Adair, Daniel McCoy & A. Fields, Judges

Court adjourned until Monday nine o'clock **present as on Saturday**

Bear Paw
Court met according to adjournment present as on Saturday their Hons SC

Bear Paw	)	Trover 1 St___
	)	
vs	)	
	)	The Court find for Deft
Feather Tiger	)	

Cah you cah te hud attendance as witness

7 days	$5.25
Tallanuturkee	5.25
Back Bows	3.25
A. Percinow	5.75
	$19.50

Execution issued 29th Nov. 1835

Monday 26th

Hirady	)	Debt killing a cow.

	)	
vs	)	
	)	Court finds for Ptff
David Miller	)	Twelve dollars. $12.00

Witnesses	
John Hodges	3.00
4 days	2.25
John Grigsby 3 days	1.50
Nancy Wahtalookah 2 days	1.50
Clab board 2 days	1.50
Sitting downs 2 days	1.50
	$9.75

The Court fine John Broward one dollar for Contempt of Court.

Court adjourned until tomorrow morning nine o'clock

Tuesday 27th

Court met according to adjournment. Present as yesterday their Hons.

Court adjourned to tomorrow nine o'clock

Wednesday 28

The Hon Court met agreeable to adjournment. Present as on yesterday

Walter S. Adair & Archy Fields having been objected to by one of the parties Geo. M. Martin & John Martin are appointed by a resolution of the Genl Council as substitutes.
The above named Judges pro tem appeared & was qualified & took their seats.

Nathan Hicks	)	Recover on bond $1,000.
	)	
vs	)	
	)	
Isaac Bushehead	)	Non Suit
Tho Foreman &	)	**The Court find for the**

Jesse Bushehead	)	
Che, nah, Sak	)	Trover to recover mare & colt
	)	
vs	)	
	)	The Court find for the Plaintiff
Akey	)	the mare & colt or the
	)	value thereof

Execution issued 1st Nov 1835

Court adjourned to tomorrow morning nine o'clock

Thursday 29th

Court met according to adjournment. Present as on yesterday their Hons SC

Sally Cilington	)	Trespass clearing within a quarter
	)	of a mile of her fields
vs	)	
	)	We the Court find for the
William Williams	)	Plaintiff all the land **under**
	)	contained within 1/4 a mile of the
	)	upper field except

½ half of the part that comes within the 1/4 of a mile of the defendant's improvement which he purchased from Bendabout and that the officers of this District where the field lies thats appoint suitable persons who are disinterested to make this decision.

On Motion ordered, that in this case Mrs Wilkyson so ___ Borrow that there be by the Sherriff of the Dist two men appointed who are disinterested to examine the ____ inspect to & determine whether there be any of the said ____ of on not and then testimony taken as the ___ present time for this Court.

The Court adjourned until 10 o'clock tomorrow.

Friday 30th October

The Court met according to adjournment. Present their Honors D McCoy, Fields & Adair

Sy__kie	)	Debt on a/ct
	)	
vs	)	
	)	Judgment for Plaintiff for three
_________	)	dollars & three dollars seventy
	)	five cents costs

Witness
James Hair 5 days—$3.75

Execution issued 2 Nov 1835

The Court adjourned until the second Monday in October next

Personally came Elizabeth Thompson and after being sworn says on oath that a certain sound filly with a small star in her forehead four years old which was sold as an Estray on this 16th Inst. Is the property of her son John Thompson who is now about and that has not traded or conveyed away in any manner this said filly to any traders whatever—

Sworn to and subscribed	)	Elizabeth Thompson her X Mark
18th July 1835	)	
David McCoy J.S.C.	)	

May it please the Court

While Bonaparte is marching his army from Elba to Paris and from Paris back to Elba innudating the whole country in blood I stand here this humble advocate of this notorious hog thief. The goats may climb to the summit of those mountains. The sheep may find on the fields below and the cattle may graze the grass off the meadow but my client are no more guilty of stealing that are hog than a toad got no tail.

Cherokee Nation

Lowry	)	Trover to recover 7 head Cattle
	)	
vs	)	
	)	
Foreman	)	The Court

Sally Timberleg as a second mortgage Thirty ___ ___ and thereto recovered
Runne cow
James Brown

Susan Tilley	)	Claim for property: no property named in the bill cannot be ascertained

Doc'r Singleton Jackson County

Major Ridge attended———8 days
Susanna Ridge do 8——

You do solemnly swear that you ___ as clerk to this Supreme Court keep as true ___ of the proceedings of said Court ______ favor or truthfully to any party whosoever

Notice

All persons indebted to the Cherokee Nation for moneys borrowed out of the National Treasury are hereby informed that the last installment will close on the _______ January 1833, & that those wishing to settle **for their lands** up will do well ____ to call on the residence of the subscriber on or before that time.

John Martin

Major Lucans in open Court that he has attended according to a summons on him to give evidence in a cause wherein Jos. Vann was Pft vs. David & Debra McNair Dfts Ahnokee Court 8 days—for last Supreme Court 14 days—for the present term 7 days: Total 39 days at 75cts $29.25—November 11th 1835.

Elijah Hicks
C,S,C

Archd Foreman $12.00 Case __________

Cherokee language to be translated

Know all men by these presnts that I Chunuliskee PL & George Miller security as holder & firmly bound unto John Ross Pl Chief of the Cherokee Nation in the final sum of Thirty dollars well & truly to be paid we find ourselves as heirs and assigns jointly & separately dated at Chickamauga Court House this 19th day of Sept. 1834

The condition of the above and is such if the above ____ Chunuliskee **is such** does appear at Red Clay on the 2nd Monday of Oct next and answers to the complaint of Lydia on a plea of killing her hogs then in that case this bond to be null & void or otherwise to remain in full force & virtue in law given from under our hands & seals the date and year above written

Witnesses Chunooliskee X L.S.
George X Miller L.S.

Index